GRAMMAR AND PUNCTUATION ESSENTIALS FOR BUSINESS COMMUNICATION

SUSAN G. THOMAS
San Jose State University

COLLEGE DIVISION South-Western Publishing Co.

Cincinnati Ohio

EB60AB
Copyright © 1992
by South-Western Publishing Co.
Cincinnati, Ohio

ISBN: 0-538-81936-7

Printed in the United States of America

2 3 4 5 6 DH 6 5 4 3 2

Acquisitions Editor: Jeanne R. Busemeyer
Production Editor: Sue Ellen Brown
Production House: Marsico Editing & Design
Cover Designer: Craig LaGesse Ramsdell
Marketing Manager: Tania Hindersman

An inescapable fact of most careers is communication—both oral and written; hence, employers are constantly looking for candidates with strong communication skills. Applying good communication skills on the job saves time, enhances company image, and increases your personal and professional credibility. You and your company will be judged by your communication skills. You will be judged not only on the content but also on your ability to use proper grammar and punctuation.

Sometimes documents aren't given a fair chance because the writer's communication skills are so poor. The reader often thinks, perhaps unconsciously, "If this person's grammar and punctuation skills are this weak, his/her ideas can't be very good either." Perhaps this kind of connection is unfair, but it is made all the time in business.

If you are reading this page, you are probably enrolled in a college or university to obtain a business degree or a degree of some kind which will allow you to seek a career-path position in business.

Any company hiring you will expect you to have good to excellent communication skills. Unfortunately, these days many students are entering the junior and senior levels of college work with extremely weak grammar and punctuation skills and a generally weak understanding of written English—the language they will use daily on the job.

It seems that the subject of grammar, including punctuation, is not being taught as rigorously in junior high schools and high schools today as it was a few decades ago. Perhaps, we have thought that these skills would automatically be "picked up" by students writing and communicating in an English-speaking environment—and that such rigorous study of and focus on grammar as a stand-alone subject is not really necessary. The re-directing of student effort to creative writing and other pursuits in place of a rigorous grammar study has, unfortunately, caused some erosion of student capability with grammar and punctuation.

Perhaps, other students were presented with grammar and punctuation lessons but did not see the immediate need or applicability at the time and so did not internalize the concepts. Students today also are not exposed to as much of the "written word" as students were a few decades ago. In their free time, many young people today are opting for non-reading activities. Few young people today pick up a book in their spare time. The continual exposure to the written word which occurred naturally a couple of decades ago, and which enhanced student capability with the language, has dropped off markedly.

For these reasons, student writing skills are slipping year by year. Many students now need additional help to strengthen their grammar and punctuation skills. At this point in their lives, students do not need an entire English course to meet this objective nor, in most cases, is such a comprehensive course practical.

Many students recognizing their weaknesses with the written word simply do not have the time to take an entire English grammar course, even if they wanted to. Most college students are extremely busy—taking a full load of classes and perhaps working part-time. Unless a grammar course is required for graduation, most students couldn't work it into their schedule—and most universities don't require such a course. What is needed, then, at this point, is a way for students to review only the basic concepts needed to write well in business.

This text was designed with the overall goal of helping you enhance your personal and professional credibility in the area of written communication. The number of concepts included here has been purposely minimized in order to meet this objective—to help students understand and learn only those concepts necessary to write correctly and punctuate properly for "real-world" writing. This minimization of concepts also helps to reduce student frustration and the sinking feeling of "overload."

It has been found that students need far more examples of a concept than are normally found in most grammar texts. Therefore, to enhance your understanding, this text includes an abundance of business examples and, in many cases, an explanation of the examples.

The text does not claim that learning grammar is easy or that little effort is required to master the subject; on the contrary, just as the mastering of any subject requires a great deal of focus and effort, English grammar is no exception. The important thing to remember as you study and learn this material is that you will be reviewing only what is necessary and that you will have the opportunity to apply what you learn every day on the job. Your correct application of grammar and punctuation as well as other communication skills can only enhance your personal credibility and career.

Susan G. Thomas

TABLE OF CONTENTS

PARTS OF SPEECH

All the words used in speaking and writing English fall into eight classes: nouns, pronouns, verbs, adjectives, adverbs, prepositions, conjunctions, and interjections.

Following is a description of each of the eight parts of speech plus examples of each and how they are used.

NOUN

The name of a person, place, thing, quality, concept, or action

person
Diana, sister, architect

place
Newark, home, park, school

thing
desk, computer, book, building, hair, table

quality
honesty, sincerity, patience

concept
beauty, truth, love

action
writing, speaking, dancing (unless preceded by a *to be* verb form—*is writing, will be speaking, were dancing;* in these cases, the words are not nouns, but verbs)

Paul's **report** was read thoroughly by his **manager**.

Please write me your **impressions** of the **meeting**.

We made a **comparison** of company **sales** by **product** for this **year** and last **year**.

I need a **report** of monthly **production** in **units** for this **quarter**.

Practice and In-Class Exercises

Note: Answers to all practice exercises can be found at the back of the book.

Exercise 1 (Practice)
Identifying Nouns

Circle all of the nouns in the following sentences.

1. I should probably take notes of the conversation.

2. One branch manager told me that highly specialized software is important.

3. Interest is paid on the monthly balance.

4. Anyone involved with computers knows how much time can be saved with their use.

5. We should read the literature before we make a decision.

6. For many years, we have focused on distinction and fashion in our advertising campaigns.

7. If you have any good ideas, give me a call.

8. There are several important advantages to this system.

9. Unfortunately, the new format sacrifices user friendliness for more elegant design.

10. This type of account is not the best plan for everyone.

Exercise 1 (In Class)
Identifying Nouns

1. His memo requests that we study the problem with the X-250 line.

2. Walt suggested on-the-job training to give new hires a broad view of the division.

3. These three PC's were sent out for repairs last month.

4. Steve asked me to complete the report without help.

5. The analysis describes our present marketing philosophy.

6. If you can't picture the idea, don't feel bad.

7. Honesty is a character trait my manager believes in strongly.

8. Kathy had several good ideas to increase sales that I'm sure Jay will want to consider.

9. Our new product is designed for people who want status.

10. The seminar will emphasize interpersonal communication.

11. Reliability, support, and service are becoming more and more important to customers.

12. Although we are a major vendor, we face competition from 39 other vendors.

VERB

A word [or group of words] telling either what action the noun/subject is performing or linking it to a word/words that describe or rename the noun/subject.

If you can picture action in the word, the verb is called an *action verb*. Verbs are always expressed in a time context—basically, past, present, or future.

Mary **ran** out of the room when she **heard** the news.

Joseph **typed** the report while I **waited**.

Tom always **speaks** effectively when he **gives** presentations.

If you can't picture action as in the preceding sentences, the verb is performing a linking function using some form of the verb *to be* (in most cases) and is either describing the subject or *renaming* the subject.

Various forms of *to be* include:

is	shall be
are	will be
was	shall have been
were	will have been

Here a *to be* form links the noun/subject to a word that describes the subject:

My manager **is** intelligent.

Is links the noun/subject *manager* to a word that describes him/her—*intelligent*.

His tie **is** red.

Is links the noun/subject *tie* to a word that describes the tie—*red*.

Bobby's report **was** lengthy.

Was, another form of *to be*, links the noun/subject *report* to a word that describes the report—*lengthy*.

The meeting **will be** long.

Will be, another form of *to be*, links the noun/subject *meeting* to a word that describes the meeting—*long*.

PARTS OF SPEECH

The linking verb can also link the noun/subject to a noun that *renames* the subject:

My manager **is** Bob.

Is links the noun/subject to a word that renames him. *Manager* and *Bob* are one and the same.

Donna **has been** my friend for two years.

Has been, another form of *to be*, links the noun/subject, *Donna*, to a word that renames her—*friend*.

Mr. James **will be** our representative at the April 3 meeting.

Will be, another form of *to be,* links the noun/subject *Mr. James* to a word that renames him—*representative*.

Other linking verbs are:

seem	smell
appear	feel
taste	look

These verbs link the subject to either a word that describes the subject or to a noun that renames the subject, just like the *to be* verb does.

John **seems** tired.

Seems links *John* to a word that describes him—*tired*.

Debbie **appeared** tense.

Appeared links *Debbie* to a word that describes her—*tense*.

The steak **will taste** good.

Will taste links the noun/subject *steak* to a word that describes it—*good*.

Bonnie **felt** proud of her accomplishment.

Felt links the noun/subject *Bonnie* to a word that describes her—*proud*.

HELPING VERBS

A few verbs have a specialized function called *helping* and usually appear in front of an action verb.

These *helping* (or *auxiliary*) verbs are as follows:

have	will	can
has	would	could
had	shall	may
been	should	might
be	must	

If any of these forms appear singly or in combination in front of an action verb, *all parts together* constitute the *verb phrase*.

We **should have been depreciating** this equipment.

The proposal **must be submitted** by January 7, 1991.

The report **could have been taken** by Maurice to the conference.

Five employees **will be staying** late to finish[1] the graphics for the report.

The entire staff **will be notified** tomorrow.

We **might have considered** more alternatives before we made a decision.

---

[1]**Note:** To + verb (such as *to walk, to discuss, to suggest,* etc.) is **never** the verb. This construction is called an *infinitive* and comes from a larger group called *verbals*. (See the glossary for a definition of an infinitive.)

Practice and In-Class Exercises

Note: Answers to all practice exercises can be found at the back of the book.

Exercise 2 (Practice)
Identifying Verbs

Underline with two lines all the verbs in the following sentences. Be sure to include helping verbs. Mark linking verbs *LV*.

1. Charlene takes our deposit to the bank every day.

2. Although they can be extremely helpful, computers can't do everything.

3. Will you mail your remittance today?

4. Mrs. Morris read the new procedures at yesterday's meeting.

5. Tom sent me to the factory to check out the difficulty.

6. The interviewer will ask you about your work history.

7. It is important to work well with others.

8. I felt that he was evaluating me from the moment that I walked in.

9. In January, I will have been working here three years.

10. The duties that I perform now take all of my time.

11. No one at headquarters has done a better job.

12. The invoice for the last three shipments is incorrect.

13. Ignore the advice of Mr. Jamison—he just likes to talk.

14. Sixty per cent of our quota was achieved this month.

15. Half of the parking spaces in this row are available.

16. We are assuming a unit price of $5.99.

Exercise 2 (In Class)
Identifying Verbs

Underline with two lines all the verbs in the following sentences. Be sure to include helping verbs. Mark linking verbs *LV*.

1. We had several good speakers at our conference.

2. A brief discussion of theory will be included in this report.

3. All of the bank tellers have had problems with John Stark.

4. Four of the five sales representatives have increased sales in their territories in the last quarter.

5. Three speeches were given at this afternoon's marketing session.

6. Most of the offices on this side of the building are still unoccupied.

7. All of the workers have gone home for the day.

8. She is one of those people who works best under pressure.

9. The money for the project must be allocated in this quarter's budget.

10. The number of bankruptcies was higher this year than last year.

11. Twenty-four boxes of computer paper were delivered last month.

12. Neither of the setbacks was very costly.

13. Nobody among the trainees seems capable of supervising such an important project.

14. Jim Bailey wanted to perform well in his new job.

15. Office machinery must be covered and carefully protected.

16. Banks and thrifts could be headed toward a severe liquidity crisis with weak earnings.

ADJECTIVE

A word that describes (or modifies) a noun or pronoun. Adjectives answer the questions *what kind? how many? which one? how much?* or *whose?* They usually are placed **before** a noun, but not always. When a form of *to be* is the verb in the sentence, the adjective follows the verb and, thus, the noun.

Here is a small sample of words that normally function as **adjectives**:

tall	incompetent	inefficient	green
short	energetic	thick	shiny
young	terrible	boring	twenty
old	solid	bright	dark
successful	demanding	unreasonable	sour

A, an, the form a special group of adjectives called *articles.*

> *LV   adj—how many?*

She will be **20** on her next birthday.

20 is an adjective but does not precede the noun. It is used after a linking verb to describe *she*.

> *how   what*
> *many? kind?*

He wore **a red** tie.

> *what   how   what*
> *kind?   many? kind?*

The **successful** executive drove **a shiny, new** car.

> *whose?   which one?*

Marsha's report was on **the** desk.

> *which   how   what*
> *one?   many? kind?*

The manager gave **an interesting** presentation.

> *how   what   what*
> *many? kind?   kind?*

Prepare **a line** chart to show **monthly sales** totals.

Here, *sales totals* could be considered the entire noun, but for the purposes of this text, consider **sales** to be an adjective telling what kind of *totals*.

Quality graphics are **essential** to **effective report** writing.

Quality—what kind of graphics?

essential—what kind of graphics? Note that this adjective **follows** the linking verb.

effective—what kind of writing?

report—what kind of writing?

Again, the noun could be *report writing*, but, for the purposes of this text, consider **report** to be an adjective.

Jan Taylor, **the new** member of **the advisory** committee, has been an employee for **seven** years.

the —article tells, which one?

new—which one?

the—which one?

advisory—what kind of committee?

seven—how many years?

Note: *employee* is a noun that renames *Jan Taylor*, connected by the linking verb *has been*.

It is **the only water-repellent**, **snag-proof**, and **inexpensive** material **available**.

the—article tells, which one?

only—how many?

water-repellent—what kind?

snag-proof—what kind?

Note that some adjectives consist of two words, but they count as **one** adjective.

inexpensive—what kind?

available—what kind of?

Occasionally, a word that would normally be an adjective, like *three*, must serve as the sentence subject, taking a noun function:

Three of the pages are missing.

Here, *three* must serve as the sentence subject because *pages* appears in a prepositional phrase. The sentence subject can never be in a prepositional phrase. (See the glossary for a definition of prepositions.)

If the sentence had read:

>   **Three** pages are missing.

pages would have been the subject, and **three** would have been an adjective because *pages* is not now in a prepositional phrase as in the previous example.

Special rule for *a*:

A and *an* cannot be used interchangeably. You must use *an* in front of words that begin with a vowel sound:

an opening remark	an 8-hour job
an honest woman[2]	an average applicant
an unusual assignment	an everyday occurrence
an early departure	

This is wrong:

>   The following is **a official** announcement.

An must be used in front of *official* because of the *o* vowel sound on *official*.

This is correct:

>   The following is **an official** announcement.

The only exception to using *an* before a vowel sound is when the first letter has a long *u* sound. In this case, precede the word with *a*:

a union	a unique contribution
a unanimous vote	a universal belief
a usual procedure	a usable idea

---

[2]**Note:** Although *h* isn't a vowel, the *h* is not pronounced on this word. The following *o* is the sound heard when *honest* is pronounced. In contrast, the *h* on *horse* is pronounced, so *a* is the proper article before *horse*.

Practice and In-Class Exercises

Note: Answers to all practice exercises can be found at the back of the book.

Exercise 3 (Practice)
Identifying Adjectives

Circle all adjectives in the following sentences. Adjectives answer the question, *which one? how many? what kind? how much?* or *whose?* Count articles *(a, an, the)* as adjectives.

1. Our pricing structure is the result of several internal and external factors.

2. One problem we have had is with attendance.

3. Increasing pressure from the competition has forced us to react with price cuts.

4. Much excitement was generated over the incident.

5. Jan gave a stimulating presentation that kept everyone's interest.

6. The department is looking for an articulate, dependable, and personable receptionist.

7. This improved model is safe, nonpolluting, and durable.

8. Three projects have been delayed due to internal workload problems and overly optimistic scheduling.

9. Further study will be done before we can make a definite commitment.

10. These tables are perfect for the conference room.

11. The attached report summarizes investment performance for the first quarter of the fiscal year.

12. The three programmers came to the wrong conclusion.

13. Donald made a supreme sacrifice when he agreed to work on Saturday.

14. The company-owned computer equipment has been depreciated for five years.

15. The brochure was very colorful and informative.

16. The compounded annual growth rate is forecast at 29%.

Exercise 3 (In Class)
Identifying Adjectives

Circle all adjectives in the following sentences. Adjectives answer the question, *which one? how many? what kind? how much?* or *whose?* Count articles *(a, an, the)* as adjectives.

1. We have always employed a two-tier distribution strategy.

2. Both men are very conservative marketing managers.

3. This report contains three sections of interest to us.

4. Our well-known label is red and blue.

5. A frequent complaint is that we have few openings for the number of applicants.

6. Brandon's sales report was presented at the morning meeting.

7. Here is a status report of 14 ongoing projects.

8. Four ideas for improved effectiveness were implemented.

9. Our primary distribution channel consists of 200 retail stores.

10. Martha is rather irresponsible and has irritated several people with her immaturity.

11. Joe said that this problem has come up before.

12. Our Christmas catalogue was mailed yesterday to current customers.

13. Final approval of the project will likely be given tomorrow.

14. Our goal has always been to provide our customers with the most advanced and useful personal computers in the world.

15. We were discouraged when we saw that we had received fewer orders this month.

16. Education is a vital aspect of an effective employee retention program.

ADVERB

A word that modifies a verb, adjective, or other adverb.

Adverbs do not modify nouns. Adverbs answer the questions *when? how? where? to what extent?* Adverbs often end in *ly*.

adverb   *adverb*
how?   *how?*
She typed the report **quickly** and **accurately**.

These adverbs modify the verb typed **not** the noun report. It's not report quickly but typed quickly. Adverbs do not modify nouns.

adverb—to what extent conscientious?
She is **extremely** conscientious.

The adverb **extremely** modifies the adjective *conscientious,* **not** the pronoun she. *Adverbs do not modify nouns or pronouns.*

Following the meeting, Sherry **sincerely** congratulated me on my presentation.

The adverb **sincerely** modifies the verb *congratulated,* **not** the noun *Sherry.*

First carefully analyze our position in the market, **then** write a report covering our status and your suggestions.

First tells, when? and modifies the verb *analyze.*

carefully tells, how? and modifies the verb *analyze.*

then tells, when? and modifies the verb *write.*

The president **completely** reorganized our department.

completely tells, to what extent? and modifies the verb *reorganized.*

Sales were **slightly** higher this quarter than last quarter.

slightly tells, to what extent? and modifies the adjective *higher.* Notice that both the adverb *(slightly)* and the adjective *(higher)* follow the noun and are connected to it by the linking verb *were.*

We have **consistently** used the same material to manufacture this part.

consistently tells, to what extent? and modifies the verb *used.*

David is **always** prepared for his clients.

always tells, to what extent? and modifies the verb *prepared.*

Mr. Martin **quickly** but **politely** answered a **very** difficult question.

quickly tells, how? and modifies the verb *answered*.

politely tells, how? and modifies the verb *answered*.

very tells, to what extent? and modifies the adjective *difficult* .

Here is a small sample of words that normally function as adverbs:

individually—how?

accidentally—when? or how?

privately—how?

publicly—how?

instantly—when?

cooperatively—how?

hastily—how?

aggressively—how?

immediately—when?

logically—how?

exceedingly—to what extent?

consistently— to what extent? how?

almost [preceding an adjective]—to what extent?

entirely—to what extent?

then [when modifying a verb]—when?

accurately—how?

hurriedly—how?

courteously—how?

imaginatively—how?

very—to what extent?

rather— to what extent?

entirely—to what extent?

seldom—when?

quite—to what extent?

soon—when?

now—when?

too—to what extent?

most [preceding an adjective or other adverb]—to what extent?

first [when modifying a verb] —when?

tomorrow—when?

EXPLETIVES PART 1

Occasionally, a sentence will begin with a word like *there*. In some instances, *there* is not an adverb:

> **There** are many problems with this report.

In this sentence, **There** does not really answer the question, *where?* Neither is it the sentence subject.

In this case, *there* is an **expletive** or filler word—*There is...* and *There are...* are simply ways to get the sentence started. They should be avoided, however, since they produce weak sentences—weak because the beginning word means nothing. It is better to say:

> This report has several problems.

Another example of an expletive beginning:

> **There** are several reasons why Joe left the company.

Reword for a stronger sentence:

> Joe left the company for several reasons.

Remember...expletives are never sentence subjects.

Practice and In-Class Exercises

Note: Answers to all practice exercises can be found at the back of the book.

Exercise 4 (Practice)
Identifying Adverbs

Circle all adverbs. Adverbs answer the questions, *how? to what extent? when?* or *where?* Adverbs describe *verbs, adjectives,* or other *adverbs*—never nouns. Draw an arrow to the word the adverb describes. Some sentences may contain no adverbs.

1. The effective speaker pronounces words clearly.

2. The latest order was carefully printed on very expensive stationery.

3. The new bookkeeping software automatically bills, posts, and maintains inventory control.

4. We must change our advertising appeal immediately, or we will surely lose a large portion of the market.

5. A satisfied employee won't be easily lured away by our competitors.

6. Our equipment is too old.

7. The applicant responded somewhat nervously to the interviewer's questions.

8. Intense price competition is already evident.

9. He performs his duties exceptionally well.

10. I scarcely knew him when he was promoted to manager.

11. I have never been to Philadelphia.

12. Proofread carefully all data entries.

13. She often travels to Chicago on business.

14. Customers need to feel that their needs are handled effectively and efficiently.

15. No two people are completely alike.

16. Our increased income has been severely eroded by federal taxes.

Exercise 4 (In Class)

Identifying Adverbs

Circle all adverbs. Adverbs answer the questions, *how? to what extent? when?* or *where?* Adverbs describe *verbs, adjectives,* or other *adverbs*—never nouns. Draw an arrow to the word the adverb describes. Some sentences may contain no adverbs.

1. She is very content with her current position.

2. We certainly hope you will stay for the meeting.

3. We must maintain a highly controlled security system.

4. As the industry evolves, we will be increasingly challenged to meet market demands.

5. Prices this year are substantially higher than last year's.

6. Dave responded quickly to the criticism.

7. Flextime has been implemented successfully at other plants.

8. Frank was rather reluctant to suggest any improvements.

9. Few employees had read the directions accurately.

10. Our return on total assets has improved substantially.

11. Sandra generously offered me the use of her office.

12. The June project was temporarily postponed due to insufficient funding.

13. Laura, my assistant, had originally planned to complete the typing by noon.

14. Don relied very heavily on my interpretation of the contract to write a rebuttal.

15. Only two staff members had read the minutes of the meeting.

16. Each management team should regularly set and monitor individual employee goals.

PRONOUN

A word that substitutes for a noun and is used to provide efficiency and variety in a sentence.

The pronouns that could replace nouns or serve as sentence subjects are

all	any	anyone	anything
both	each	either	everyone
few	he	I	it
many	most	neither	no one
nobody	none	none	one
several	she	some	somebody
someone	that	these	they
this	those	we	what
whoever	you		

Everyone should contribute at least one idea.

We cannot agree on a solution.

One of the chapters is missing.

Some of the employees took an extra day of vacation.

None of the members came to the Christmas party.

That is a good suggestion.

Nothing angers me more than **someone** who isn't dependable.

The pronouns that could function as adjectives are

all	any	both	each
either	few	her	her
his	many	most	my
one	other	our	some
that	their	these	this
those	whose	your	

When a pronoun serves as an adjective (appearing in front of a noun or after a linking verb and answers one of the *adjective questions)*, technically it is no longer a pronoun. Consider it an **adjective**.

how
many?   *whose?*
Some managers provide **their** employees with performance incentives.

        how
        many?
I objected for **several** reasons.

    which
    ones?
All of **those** terminals need repair.

       how
       many?
Stan has developed **many** brilliant solutions.

     whose?   *whose?*
She grabbed **her** coat and ran to **her** car.

how
many?   *whose?*
Few infractions escape **my** manager.

which   *how*
one?   *much?*
Either idea could be implemented with **some** success.

Several pronouns could be turned into adjectives by adding *'s* to them:

     whose guess?
What will happen is **anyone's** guess.

whose idea?
Nobody's idea will be ignored.

    whose coat?
I found **somebody's** coat in the lobby.

       whose health?
Please smoke outside for **everyone's** health.

      whose feelings?
Such a comment could hurt **someone's** feelings.

Note: Sometimes a pronoun that would normally be an adjective, like *several*, must serve as the sentence subject because the true subject of the sentence is in a prepositional phrase.

Several of our employees were late to work on Tuesday.

Normally, *several* would be an adjective telling how many. In this case, *employees* appears in a prepositional phrase, *of our employees*. Since the subject of a sentence **can never be** in a prepositional phrase, **several** must now be the subject and can no longer be considered an adjective here. If the sentence had been

Several employees were late to work on Tuesday

Several would have been an adjective modifying *employees*.

A few pronouns are considered *possessive* and used to describe something that belongs to a noun:

ours yours mine theirs its

Note that **no apostrophe** is ever used with these forms to denote possession—they are already in the possessive form.

The idea was **theirs**. Whose idea? (**never** *their's*)

The coat is **mine**. Whose coat? (**never** *who's*)

Which desk is **yours**? (**never** *your's*)

The company had **its** books audited. (**never** *it's*)

The following pronoun forms are used in prepositional phrases:

me you them us

Give the report to Bob or **me**.

Not I. You would never say

Give the report to I.

Don't let the other name in front confuse you—**me** is still correct. The prepositional phrase is *to Bob or me*.

The birthday card is from all of **us**.

Prepositional phrase is *of us*.

He gave **you** and **me** the best assignments.

You and *me* are called **indirect objects**. This is a common structure in English. The sentence really means

He gave the best assignments to **you** and **me**.

The true structure shows that *you* and *me* appear in a prepositional phrase beginning with *to*. He didn't give you and me, he gave the best assignments *to* you and me.

EXPLETIVES PART 2

It can be another **expletive** word with no meaning. The constructions are usually *It is...* or *It was....*

> **It** was difficult to make a decision in this case.

It here is not a true pronoun substituting for a noun, or referring to a noun somewhere else in the sentence. *It* is merely a filler word, a way to get the sentence started.

Occasionally an expletive beginning sounds better than any other construction.

With expletive beginning:

> It was difficult to make a decision in this case.

Without expletive beginning—words re-arranged, a little more cumbersome to read:

> To make a decision in this case was difficult.
>
> or
>
> A decision in this case was difficult to make.

Whatever construction you choose, remember that normally sentences with an expletive beginning are weaker because the first word in the sentence doesn't mean anything. However, as in the previous example, the expletive beginning occasionally makes the sentence *less* awkward.

Practice and In-Class Exercises

Note: Answers to all practice exercises can be found at the back of the book.

Exercise 5 (Practice)

Identifying Pronouns

Circle all of the pronouns substituting for nouns in the following sentences. Do not circle pronouns used as adjectives. Some sentences contain no pronouns.

1. Anyone interested in a ride to the picnic should call me.

2. He gave me three good reasons why we cannot implement my idea.

3. It is not a matter of time; it is a matter of priority.

4. Bring your ideas to our next staff meeting.

5. I can't understand your point.

6. None of the results happened as he had predicted.

7. He spoke for 15 minutes and presented some good ideas to us.

8. Her purse was found in the lobby.

9. Few of you understand the importance of the joint venture.

10. It isn't anyone's fault.

11. I convinced her to attend the meeting.

12. We need to replace those chairs before additional purchases are made.

13. The Los Angeles office, expanded three years ago, now houses 500 employees.

14. The sales representative selling the most this month will receive a special bonus in December.

15. As Pete walked to his car, he realized that he would be late for his dinner appointment.

16. We are increasingly using teleconferencing for employee training.

Exercise 5 (In Class)
Identifying Pronouns

Circle all of the pronouns substituting for nouns in the following sentences. Do not circle pronouns used as adjectives. Some sentences contain no pronouns.

1. David said he needed extra time to finish the project.

2. Diane noted the difference in costs.

3. When we introduced the new software, many employees responded enthusiastically.

4. Anyone who would like more information should see Jan.

5. We must accept their proposal by noon tomorrow, or we will lose a valuable opportunity.

6. They really have only two options.

7. I noticed that several employees were late today.

8. He left his analysis on my desk in a manila envelope.

9. All of the staff members agreed that we should institute flextime.

10. Who would like to take this assignment?

11. Everyone must attend one session of the conference.

12. That remark was overheard by several of us.

13. We received two shipments yesterday, but both are incomplete.

14. It is our intention to offer the position to Donna.

15. I agree with you on that point.

PREPOSITION

A word used to show the relationship between a noun or pronoun that follows it and a previous word in the sentence. The preposition plus the noun or pronoun (and any intervening words) form what is called a **prepositional phrase**.

Common phrase structures are

(1) preposition + noun (or pronoun)

for Elliot; to us; from today; about noon

(2) preposition + adjective + noun

from the computer; despite Fran's remarks

(3) preposition + adjective + adjective + noun

after the first quarter; without a logical reason

(4) preposition + noun + coordinating conjunction + noun:

in this office and company; concerning recent trends and projections; for better or worse

Here are some common prepositions and how they might look in a sentence ·

about	about the report, about you, about five reasons,	*against*	against all odds, against the wall,
above	above the clouds, above all, above the picture,	*along*	along the shore, along the paper, along the edge,
across	across the room, across the street,	*among*	among the group, among your ideas,
*after**	after tomorrow, after the paragraph, after the speech,	*around*	around the corner, around three, around the idea,

as for	as for my opinion, as for your idea,	*by*	by the time, by noon, by his foot, by going,
at	at the time, at the corner, at the outset, at noon,	*concerning*	concerning my report, concerning his at- tendance,
because of	because of your interest, because of my concerns,	*despite*	despite the news, despite my objections,
*before**	before yesterday, before noon, before the meeting,	*down*	down the street, down the hall, down the side,
behind	behind my back, behind the desk, behind the times,	*due to*	due to recent trends, due to my absence,
below	below the surface, below standard, below the price,	*during*	during the meeting, during the discussion, during May,
beneath	beneath my dignity, beneath the table, beneath me,	*except*	except you, except this report,
beside	beside the water, beside his desk,	*for*	for a few hours, for this reason, for five days,
besides	besides you, besides my manager,	*from*	from today, from here, from my desk, from the outset,
between	between you and me, between the lines,	*in*	in three weeks, in this office, in total, in me,
beyond	beyond recognition, beyond the bounds,		
but	(meaning *except*) but him, but this page,	*into*	into the door, into three paragraphs, into Chicago,

like	like you, like this, like Mr. Johnson, like this book,	*through*	through the gate, through proper channels,
of	of the report, of the highway, of the week, of three,	*throughout*	throughout her stay, throughout the week,
off	off the wall, off his game, off the mark,	*to*	to the store, to the end, to my office,
on	on the mark, on Tuesday, on the table, on time,	*toward*	toward another, toward the window, toward you,
onto	onto the desk, onto my lap,	*under*	under consideration, under the table,
over	over the building, over my manager's head,	*underneath*	underneath her foot, underneath the floor,
near	near Mr. Watson, near the total, near the end,	*until**	until tomorrow, until July,
past	past the entrance, past my understanding,	*up*	up the street,
regarding	regarding this proposal, regarding your idea,	*upon*	upon considering, upon a final analysis,
respecting	respecting this proposal, respecting this idea,	*with*	with your approval, with my time, with his effort,
*since**	since your arrival, since yesterday, since May,	*within*	within the parameters, within the scope,
		without	without my coat, without an answer, without you,

*These words also sometimes function as **subordinate conjunctions**. If one of these words is being used as a subordinate conjunction, it will be followed by a subject/verb construction and not simply a noun or adjective/noun. Subordinate conjunctions will be discussed in the next section.

Practice and In-Class Exercises

Note: Answers to all practice exercises can be found at the back of the book.

Exercise 6 (Practice)
Identifying Prepositions

Circle each prepositional phrase in the sentences that follow.

1. In 1990, we exported 30% of our production.

2. I noticed the stack of personnel files beside his desk.

3. The memo is due in my office by noon tomorrow.

4. Suggestions for improvement must be made through proper channels.

5. Richard said he would stay with the company until July 30.

6. Sally warned me not to go over my manager's head on this issue.

7. The most effective part of the report is the analysis of next year's sales projections.

8. My plane flies into Chicago at noon on Thursday.

9. Under the previous management, we operated in a casual style.

10. With your approval, I will order three new computers from Mr. Henley.

11. We were told to respond to the contract change within three days.

12. Most of the information is in the hands of our attorneys in Chicago.

13. You need to stay for a few hours to finish the graphics for tomorrow's presentation.

14. Between you and me, I think Barbara Davis is unhappy with her new position.

15. I took the new hire to the employee lunchroom.

Exercise 6 (In Class)
Identifying Prepositions

Circle each prepositional phrase in the sentences that follow.

1. Despite the late hour, we stayed through the night to finish next year's projections.

2. Because my career is important to me, I always try to submit finished assignments on time.

3. We are considering Joan Takahashi for a position in the Accounting Department.

4. We will be visited by head office personnel on Tuesday.

5. Keep a positive tone to the end of the message.

6. All needed repairs to your computer are covered under warranty.

7. This assignment is beyond the scope of my capability.

8. Readers always read between the lines of a message.

9. Mr. Green walked into my office after lunch to announce his decision.

10. I left the office without my brief case, so I did not have the papers I needed for the dinner meeting.

11. I have noticed that my manager always listens carefully to every speaker.

12. Above all, say something of value when John asks for your opinion.

13. My manager's speech at the conference was below his usual standard.

14. There was a lot of disagreement among group members about the approach we should take.

15. To assure yourself of a ticket, mail the enclosed reservation card today.

CONJUNCTION

A word that connects words or groups of words.

Conjunctions are of three types:

- coordinate
- correlative
- subordinate

There are five common coordinating conjunctions:

and   but   or   nor   so

Coordinate conjunctions join parts of speech and grammatical constructions of the same type:

noun   *cc*   *noun*
Ms. Brown **and** Mr. Johnson were promoted.
And connects two nouns.

independent   *independent*
clause   *cc*   *clause**
They were promoted, **but** I was not.
But connects two independent clauses.

*Note: An **independent clause** must include, at minimum, a subject (noun) and verb.

Send your payment, **or** we will bill you later.
Or connects two independent clauses.

He was intelligent **and** capable.
And connects two adjectives—*intelligent, capable.*

She typed the report with speed **and** with accuracy.
And connects two prepositional phrases—*with speed, with accuracy.*

Please bring to the meeting a notebook, the report, **and** today's agenda.
And joins three nouns—notebook, report, agenda.

Terry arrived late, **so** I will have to give the presentation.
So joins two independent clauses.

Correlative conjunctions join equal parts of speech as well, but they work as pairs. The following are correlative conjunctions:

> both...and
> neither...nor
> either...or
> not only...but also
> whether...or

> **Both** Terry **and** Sandra received promotions.

Joins two nouns.

> John has gone **either** to the cafeteria **or** to the conference room.

Joins two prepositional phrases.

> **Neither** capable **nor** knowledgeable, Mr. Markham received a promotion anyway.

Joins two adjectives.

> My manager gave me **not only** criticism **but also** suggestions.

Joins two nouns. Be sure to include the **also** when you use this construction; to leave out the **also** is wrong.

This construction is useful when you want to emphasize one thing over another:

> Erin **not only** compiles the data **but also** analyzes it as well.

Subordinate conjunctions include such words as *until, since, because, although,* and *while*. They are placed before a subject and verb to create a **subordinate clause** or **dependent clause**.

The meaning implied in any subordinate conjunction creates, automatically, a subordinate idea—an idea that is less important than the idea conveyed in the independent clause within the same sentence. The subordinate clause can be placed either before or after the independent (or main) clause. The next section explains subordinate conjunctions and subordinate clauses more fully.

SUBORDINATE CLAUSES

A subordinate clause is a group of words containing a subject and verb but which cannot stand alone as a complete thought. The reason the clause cannot stand alone is because the first word of the clause makes the thought sound incomplete by itself. There are three types of subordinate clauses—adverb, adjective, and noun.

Adverb Clause

An adverb clause begins with a subordinate conjunction and is followed by a subject and verb and, perhaps, other words. This group of words forms a thought, but because the words begin with a subordinate conjunction, the thought is subordinate or dependent on a more important idea. A subordinate conjunction before a subject and verb automatically *subordinates* or makes *subordinate* the thought to another, more important thought in the sentence. Hence, an adverb clause cannot stand alone as a sentence. It sounds incomplete when spoken. When the subordinate clause is spoken aloud, and when the thought appears first in the sentence, the subordinate thought leaves you hanging—your *ear* waits to hear a more important thought to follow. If the subordinate conjunction were removed, the thought could stand alone as a sentence. An adverb clause is often simply referred to as a **subordinate clause** or **dependent clause**.

There are many subordinate conjunctions. Following are some of the more common ones and examples of how they might be used to create subordinate ideas.

Note that each example (1) begins with a subordinate conjunction, (2) contains a subject and verb, and (3) sounds incomplete. Each example is called a **subordinate clause**, and each clause serves an adverb function, answering one of the tests of an adverb—Why? How? When? Where? or To what extent?

after*   after we submit the report,
after the meeting was adjourned,
after the results were obtained,

although   although we did not agree,
although productivity improved in March,
although we are in a service industry,

as   as I gave my presentation,
as Mr. Davidson began his remarks,
as I answered the telephone,

as I was walking to the parking lot,
as they were talking,
as reports were coming in,

as if   as if he heard me,
as if we knew the answer,
as if Mr. Katz could read my mind,

as long as   as long as the company has been in business,
as long as we have only three assistants,
as long as I can remember,

as soon as   as soon as we receive the results,
as soon as I get the promotion,
as soon as Ms. Jamison was promoted,
as soon as we produce 5,000 units,

as though   as though we hadn't heard,
as though his remarks didn't hurt me,
as though he didn't know any better,

because   because I disagreed with the concept,
because my manager likes me,
because we were afraid of the competition,
because the report was not favorable,

before*   before I met you,
before Mr. Johnson went on vacation,
before the claim was filed,

even if   even if my manager approves,
even if it doesn't rain,
even if I get a raise,

even though   even though we did submit the report on time,
even though the shipment went out on Monday,
even though Mr. Johnson got promoted,

if   if I had only known,
if Jim submits the report three days late,
if you want my advice,
if profits don't improve by January 1,
if Bob and Tom arrive by noon,

provided   provided we know of the meeting,
provided we can accomplish the task by Tuesday,
provided the report is short,

*since**   since you asked,
since we have already spent two hours on the report,
since I arrived here,

so that   so that we can get the report in on time,
so that I could make a good impression,

unless   unless I know in advance,
unless our market share increases,
unless Mr. Thompson gets a raise,
unless the rain stops,
unless the idea is accepted by everyone,

*until**   until she gives the word,
until we become more efficient,
until the company develops a new philosophy,

when   when four more people arrive,
when this meeting began,
when the competition hears of this,
when I received my performance appraisal,

whenever   whenever my manager starts to speak,
whenever it rains,
whenever the meeting lasts more than one hour,

wherever   wherever you go,
wherever you find support,

while while I was working on my report,
while they were having lunch,
while Jan was in Mr. Harwood's office,

why why we gave no response,
why Mr. Butler went on vacation at a time like this,

Again, all of these examples are **subordinate clauses** because they each

1. begin with a subordinate conjunction

2. contain both a subject and verb (so they are not phrases)

3. cannot stand alone as an independent idea or an independent clause

*These words also sometimes function as prepositions. If one of these words is being used as a preposition, it will be followed by a noun or adjective/noun, or adjective/adjective noun. If one of these words is being used as a subordinate conjunction, it will be followed by a subject/verb construction and not simply a noun or adjective/noun:

Prep clause

prep   noun
I didn't find out the results **until yesterday**.

Sub clause

sc   s   v
I didn't find out the results **until I received yesterday's mail.**

Prep clause

prep noun
Since noon, it has been raining.

Sub clause

sc   s   hv   v
Since my idea was implemented, sales have increased 13%.

Notice that *Since my idea* looks like a prepositional phrase. However, if you label it as such, what noun goes with the verb, *was implemented?* No words are left to go with *was implemented*. What was implemented? Therefore, *Since my idea* cannot be a prepositional phrase here. *Since* must be a subordinate conjunction, *idea* must be the clause subject, and *was implemented* must be the verb of the subordinate clause.

If the subordinate or dependent clause begins the sentence, follow it with a comma:

Whenever staff meetings last more than an hour, Tom gets restless.

If the subordinate clause occurs in the middle of the sentence, set it off with commas:

Several of us, **because we heard the report**, expressed concern about the future.

If the subordinate clause appears at the end of the sentence, **do not** separate the main clause from the subordinate clause with a comma.

My manager always gets restless **whenever the meeting lasts more than one hour**.

We continued to work **as though we hadn't heard**.

I argued vehemently **because I disagreed with the concept**.

I have worked in three different positions **since I arrived here**.

I won't have to work Saturdays **as soon as I get the promotion**.

I looked up the figures **as they were talking**.

Practice and In-Class Exercises

Note: Answers to all practice exercises can be found at the back of the book.

Exercise 7 (Practice)
Identifying Conjunctions

Mark all coordinating conjunctions with a **cc** and all subordinate conjunctions with **sc**. Bracket the entire subordinate clause. Underline the subject of the subordinate clause with one line, the verb with two lines.

1. We will settle your account when you fulfill the terms of the contract.

2. You will be paid a monthly salary of $3,000 and will receive the standard benefit package.

3. Bring your notes, ideas, and calculator to the next meeting.

4. Although I have been here only one month, I have met 50 people.

5. As you know, Jackie has been in charge of that department for the last two years.

6. Until I hear from you, I will not forward my response.

7. If the changes are acceptable to the rest of the committee, we'll incorporate them into the contract.

8. Unless business improves soon, we will be forced to make cutbacks.

9. While I was walking to the car, I noticed Mr. Jamison in the hall.

10. Although my vacation is still months away, I can't help thinking about it often.

11. Bob and Terry volunteered for the two-month assignment.

12. Joe or I will spend ten minutes answering your questions.

13. Several ideas were suggested, but my manager didn't like any of them.

14. As soon as the revised projections are ready, please send them to me.

15. David and I have been working on the budget since noon.

Exercise 7 (In Class)
Identifying Conjunctions

Mark all coordinating conjunctions with a **cc** and all subordinate conjunctions with **sc**. Bracket the entire subordinate clause. Underline the subject of the subordinate clause with one line, the verb with two lines.

1. When you have thoroughly interpreted your research, outline your approach.

2. If you guide your audience carefully toward your conclusion, you are more likely to keep their attention.

3. Even though Mr. Barrett seems to have made up his mind, be alert for the opportunity to make another suggestion.

4. Although your report is very short, I feel you have done a good job of explaining your position.

5. So that we can get the results to the vice-president's office today, would you please work through the lunch hour?

6. I think we should hold our conference at the Lamont Hotel or at the Hilton International.

7. Because many members will bring spouses, the Lamont Hotel has an advantage.

8. In the first week of operation, I hired two secretaries.

9. After three months of searching, I found the software package for our needs.

10. As I mentioned in my letter of October 24, we are concerned with two of the contract provisions.

11. We cannot draw any conclusions from this data unless we find something more conclusive.

12. Sales in all southwest and northwest regions increased from 10% to 30% in the second quarter.

13. If you would like us to consider you for the position, submit your resume and application to Roberta Saunders by February 1.

14. I called Synatek yesterday to see when we will receive copies of their engineering reports.

15. We will kick off the advertising campaign in February since we obtained adequate funding.

Adjective Clause

Another type of subordinate clause is the adjective clause. This type of clause begins with a relative pronoun—usually *who, which,* or *that.* This clause has a subject and verb but cannot stand alone as a main thought. An adjective clause answers one of the adjective questions, such as *which one? how many?* or *what kind?*

In most adjective clauses, the pronoun beginning the clause is also the subject of the clause. If the beginning word is not the subject as well, the word will usually be a subordinate conjunction. (The word *that* can be either a relative pronoun or subordinate conjunction. If it also serves as the subject of the clause, it is a relative pronoun. If it is **not** the subject of the clause and the pronoun *which* could not be substituted in its place, *that* is considered to be a subordinate conjunction.)

If the adjective clause begins with *that,* the word will sometimes be omitted. Some writers feel that a sentence is easier to understand when *that* is omitted in some adjective clauses:

A man **I know** works 7 days a week, 365 days a year.

As you look for adjective clauses in sentences, be sure to *mentally* put **that** back into the sentence:

A man **(that) I know** works 7 days a week, 365 days a year.

That I know is an adjective clause that answers the question, *which one? which man?*

(that)   relative pronoun

I—subject of clause

know—verb of clause

The three people **who arrived late** sat in the back.

The clause answers the question, which ones?—which three people?

who—relative pronoun and subject of clause

arrived—verb of clause

The man **who directs the clinic** is Mr. Johnstone.

The clause answers the question, which one?—which man?

who—relative pronoun and subject of clause

directs—verb of clause

The argument **that we should open another location** is a good one.
The clause answers the question, which one?—which argument?

that—subordinate conjunction (cannot substitute *which*)
we—subject of clause
should open—verb of clause

The town **which borders the river** is growing rapidly.
The clause answers the question, which town?
which—relative pronoun and subject of clause
borders—verb of clause

The change **that Ms. Jackson approved yesterday** will go into effect on Monday.
The clause answers the question, which change?
that—relative pronoun (meaning *which*)
Ms. Jackson—subject of clause
approved—verb of clause

The five reports **which were typed this afternoon** were sent to the vice-president for final O.K.
The clause answers the question, which reports?
which—relative pronoun and subject of clause
were typed—verb phrase of clause

Anyone **who is courteous** has an advantage.
Answers the question, which one?
who—relative pronoun and subject of clause
is—linking verb of clause

Noun Clause

A noun clause is another type of subordinate clause. It has a subject and verb and usually begins with *that* or *what*. Because the clause begins with a subordinate conjunction, the clause cannot stand alone. A noun clause answers the question, *what?*

Mrs. Markham said **that prices would rise soon**.
A noun clause answering what Mrs. Markham said.
that—subordinate conjunction
prices—subject of noun clause
would rise—verb of noun clause

The vice-president remarked **that our staff is highly competent**.
A noun clause answering what the vice-president remarked.
that—subordinate conjunction
staff—subject of noun clause
is—linking verb of noun clause

I knew **that a promotion for Esther was inevitable**.
A noun clause answering the question, what I knew.
that—subordinate conjunction
promotion—subject of noun clause
was—linking verb of noun clause

I don't know yet **what we will do with the old personal computers**.
A noun clause answering the question, what I don't know.
what—relative pronoun
we—subject noun clause
will do—verb phrase of noun clause

Practice and In-Class Exercises

Note: Answers to all practice exercises can be found at the back of the book.

Exercise 8 (Practice)
Identifying Adjective Clauses

Circle all adjective clauses in the following sentences. These clauses will begin with *who, which,* or *that.* Underline the subject of the clause with one line and the verb of the clause with two lines. In several of the clauses, the *who, which,* or *that* also serves as the subject of the clause. Since adjective clauses, like adjectives, modify nouns, what noun does the clause modify? Does the adjective clause make this noun more specific? If so, the clause is essential (must be included in the sentence for proper understanding); if not, the clause is nonessential (clause could be removed without changing the meaning of the sentence).

1. The car that is parked by the front door belongs to the vice-president.

2. We will pay the bill that arrived yesterday.

3. The people in our office who won the prize will get a bonus.

4. Our office, which is located on First Street, has been open since 1969.

5. Air that is polluted is bad for you.

6. The monthly reports that came in after 5 p.m. will not be read until Monday.

7. The person who works hard will move up rapidly in this company.

8. Donna Roberts, who has considerable experience in selling new product ideas, will be the featured speaker this evening.

9. The new policy that prohibits smoking indoors was received happily by 90% of the staff.

10. Four refrigerators are needed for our new cafeteria, which is scheduled for a July 1 completion.

11. Gregory Delgado, who has been with the company for 15 years, was recently promoted to vice-president of Finance.

12. Prepare the graphics in a way that will impress your audience.

13. Evaluate the advantages and disadvantages that we need to consider before moving ahead.

14. I have had a number of conversations with Jonathan Martin, who is in charge of our Atlanta office.

15. Jack, Nathan, and I were asked to determine the problems that we will face in introducing our new product line.

Exercise 8 (In Class)
Identifying Adjective Clauses

Circle all adjective clauses in the following sentences. These clauses will begin with *who, which,* or *that.* Underline the subject of the clause with one line and the verb of the clause with two lines. You will notice that in several of the clauses, the *who, which,* or *that* also serves as the subject of the clause. Since adjective clauses, like adjectives, modify nouns, what noun does the clause modify? Does the adjective clause make this noun more specific? If so, the clause is essential (must be included in the sentence for proper understanding); if not, the clause is nonessential (clause could be removed without changing the meaning of the sentence).

1. We were asked to consider a retirement plan which would replace our existing plan.

2. Please encourage those individuals who need help to attend the writing workshop this Saturday.

3. The graphic that you showed last is the most convincing.

4. I was working at my desk when the electrician came to fix the broken outlet that I had reported.

5. The business trip that David took in May provided us with some new clients.

6. The conference room that is located at the north end of the building is the largest of the three.

7. The person who caused the accident immediately left the scene.

8. Mr. James Whitman, who was hired only recently, quit last week.

9. All employees who would like to change insurance carriers should respond in writing by May 15.

10. Our department, which had the highest sales ever for June, received a special citation.

11. We talked over all ideas which were brought up at last week's staff meeting.

12. The 5,000 tons of steel that we ordered last month arrived this morning.

13. The address that you have for me in your files is incorrect.

14. Are you aware of the many products that are offered by our competitor?

15. The decor for the office that appeals to me most is too expensive.

Exercise 9 (Practice)
Distinguishing Between Types of Subordinate Clauses

In the following sentences, circle all subordinate clauses. Mark whether the clause is an adjective, noun, or adverb type.

1. Even though we did submit the report on time, Tammy felt it needed changing.

2. Unless our market share increases, we may have to consider some cutbacks.

3. Terry and Jim made several good suggestions that would likely be implemented.

4. I was told that the company isn't currently hiring programmers.

5. The consultant made three suggestions that would improve office communications.

6. We will have to cancel the company picnic unless the rain stops.

7. Until we become more efficient, we can never hope to improve our market share.

8. My supervisor told us that we would be getting new word processing software.

9. I felt that two major design changes could cause significant problems.

10. Although I attempted to console Stephanie, she was still concerned about her performance appraisal.

Exercise 9 (In Class)
Distinguishing Between Types of Subordinate Clauses

In the following sentences, circle all subordinate clauses. Mark whether the clause is an adjective type, noun type, or adverb type.

1. The four people who arrived late today were called in to the manager's office.

2. Julian called a meeting to discuss why our office staff was having communication problems.

3. Our new office, which was recently opened in St. Louis, is currently looking for accountants and programmers.

4. I told my supervisor that I would have the data by Friday.

5. This building site was purchased when land values were low.

6. Before a decision is made, all quarterly reports will be evaluated.

7. Ryan believes that Marketing has been spending too much on data research and collection.

8. She reminded Robert that she had cleared this course of action with him weeks ago.

9. As you requested, I will phone Mr. Stassen today for final instructions.

10. We told Interstate Roofing that their repair work last month was unacceptable.

Interjection

A word conveying strong feeling or sudden emotion, usually followed by an exclamation point:

wow! ouch! oh!

Because we seldom want to show emotion to this degree in business writing, interjections are seldom used and so will not be covered further in this text.

VERBALS

A verbal is a form of a verb root but does *not* function as a verb in the sentence. When you are looking for the verb of the independent clause, it is easy to get confused when the sentence contains a verbal. Although verbals look like verbs, they are serving another function in the sentence—as either adjective, adverb, or noun.

Verbals are of four types:

- infinitive,
- gerund,
- present participle as adjective, and
- past participle as adjective.

Infinitive

The infinitive is the easiest to recognize of the four verbals: it is **to + verb root**. The infinitive never functions as a verb in the sentence. Verbs always express action (action verbs) or perform a linking function (linking verbs) in a context of time—basically, past, present, or future. An infinitive does neither.

An infinitive **seems** to express action, but the time context of past, present, or future is missing; therefore, the infinitive form cannot be a verb.

Following are several infinitives and examples of how they might be used in a sentence. Note that in each example, the infinitive is **not** the verb of the sentence:

to walk

I don't like **to walk** to the office.

Sentence verb is *do like*—infinitive is serving a noun function here, answering *what* I don't like.

to talk

She wanted **to talk** to me at noon.

Sentence verb is *wanted*—infinitive **to talk** is serving a noun function, answering *what* she wanted.

to grow

He began **to grow** weary of the project.

Sentence verb is *began*.

to consider

We were asked **to consider** three ideas.

Sentence verb is *were asked*.

to think

We are required **to think** in our jobs.

Sentence verb is *are required*.

to allow

Jim said **to allow** 15 minutes' driving time.

Sentence verb is *said*.

to follow

My manager asks all of us **to follow** directions.

Sentence verb is *asks*.

to start

We didn't want **to start** without him.

Sentence verb is *did want*.

to reorder

We decided **to reorder** supplies.

Sentence verb is *decided*.

to persuade

He tried for three hours **to persuade** me.

Sentence verb is *tried*.

to want

To want the job is not a sin. (subject here)

Sentence verb is *is*—linking verb.

to go

    He asked me **to go** to the conference.

Sentence verb is *asked*.

Remember that *to* can also be a preposition. How do you tell the difference? If *to* is being used as a preposition in the sentence, it will be followed by a *noun* and **not** by a verb root. If *to* is followed by a verb, it is an infinitive:

        to + (adj) noun—prepositional phrase

        to + verb root—infinitive

      inf   prep phrase

I wanted **to go to the meeting**.

Practice and In-Class Exercises

Note: Answers to all practice exercises can be found at the back of the book.

Exercise 10 (Practice)

Identifying Infinitives

Circle all infinitives in the following sentences (to + verb). Some sentences contain no infinitives.

1. The purpose of this report is to identify projects that are behind schedule and to recommend corrective actions.

2. If you want the order to reach Pittsburgh by Friday, you will have to send it today.

3. Our advertising seeks to demonstrate product benefits.

4. I wanted to go to the conference, but my manager selected Brian instead.

5. She tried to persuade me to change computer systems.

6. I was afraid my suggestion would only add to the problem.

7. We are not likely to use this software package until we can find a better application for it.

8. To stimulate demand, we have decided to cut the price.

9. We were surprised to find Jerry still at work after lunch.

10. Janet couldn't understand the report, but she was afraid to ask any questions.

11. I tried to think of the last time we ordered from Simpson's.

12. Now that we have cut back on our advertising, we will have to increase our personal selling.

13. Although Mr. Robertson has been the department manager for only three weeks, he is already beginning to effect several significant changes.

14. We are trying to target a market that is large and geographically dispersed.

15. You can do much to ensure the success of your proposal.

Exercise 10 (In Class)
Identifying Infinitives

Circle all infinitives in the following sentences (to + verb).

1. It is sometimes difficult to determine the best approach.

2. Your statement has been corrected to include your recent payment of $165.

3. We want to center our response on our major objection to the plan.

4. She asked us to come to her office so that she can explain the new policy.

5. I intend to complain to my manager about Monica's behavior.

6. Please try to correct the error before Jim sees it.

7. I was disappointed to learn that you are not happy here.

8. During the past three months, we have tried very hard to motivate our sales people.

9. He told me to credit my subordinate with the idea.

10. The dinner was held to honor three retiring employees.

11. It is difficult for Jane to admit that her idea to reduce turnover didn't work.

12. It is not easy to insist on high-quality work from everyone.

13. I was asked to calculate sales for May.

14. Gabriel tried to argue his position but lost.

15. Diane is always asking us to analyze the data more thoroughly before drawing conclusions.

Gerund

The gerund is a verb with an **-ing** ending used as a noun. If the **-ing** word is being used as a verb, it will have some form of *to be* in front of it. Without the *to be* form in front, the **-ing** action verb will be either a gerund (noun) or participle (adjective). If it is functioning as a gerund, the word will be either (1) the subject of the sentence, (2) the direct object, or (3) the noun in a prepositional phrase. Often the gerund is followed by related words forming a **gerund phrase**.

walking

Walking to work is good exercise.

Walking is a gerund here, performing a noun function. The entire gerund phrase, *Walking to work* is the subject of the sentence. If **walking** had been part of the verb rather than a verbal, it would have had a *to be* form in front and read *is walking, was walking, were walking,* etc. The verb in the sentence is *is,* a linking verb here.

speaking

Speaking in front of an audience will always be frightening to me.

Speaking is a gerund here. The entire gerund phrase—*speaking in front of an audience*—is the subject of the sentence. Had *speaking* been a verb rather than a verbal, the structure would have been *is speaking, had been speaking,* etc. The verb in the sentence is a linking verb, *will be.*

shopping

My favorite activity is **shopping** for a new car.

Shopping is a gerund here, **not** part of the verb. Although a form of *to be* appears in front of **shopping**, the idea is really *shopping for a new car*—an idea. *Is* is a linking verb here, linking the noun **shopping** to the subject of the sentence, *activity*. **Shopping** renames the subject, *activity*.

proofreading

Proofreading is difficult work.

Proofreading is a noun here (gerund) and also the subject of the sentence. It is not part of the verb because no form of *to be* appears in front of **Proofreading**.

If **proofreading** had been used as a verb, the sentence would read something like:

Mr. Conway **was proofreading** the report for Mr. Jamison.

The verb in the sentence is *is*—a linking verb.

swimming

I feel refreshed after **swimming** seven laps.

The gerund **swimming** is the noun in the prepositional phrase in this sentence. *After* is a preposition here. An **-ing** verb in a prepositional phrase will **always** be a gerund. The gerund phrase is *swimming seven laps.*

If **swimming** had been a verb, the sentence would have to read something like

I **was swimming** when the phone rang

The verb in the sentence is *feel*—a linking verb.

maintaining

Maintaining good customer relations will always be important.

The gerund **maintaining** plus its related words *good customer relations* serve as the subject of the sentence as well as being a noun here.

The verb in the sentence is *will be—always* is an adverb.

Had **maintaining** been used as a verb, the sentence would have read something like:

We **have been maintaining** good customer relations for five years now.

programming

I enjoy **programming** computers.

Programming is a gerund here—the gerund phrase *programming computers* is an idea used as a noun. Since the gerund phrase answers *what I enjoy,* it is considered a direct object. The verb in this sentence is *enjoy*.

Had programming been used as a verb here, the sentence would have read

I **had been programming** the computer all day when Mr. Sheldon came in.

Gerunds, then, function as **nouns** and serve as (1) the sentence subject, (2) the noun in a prepositional phrase, or (3) a direct object telling *what* after the verb.

Practice and In-Class Exercises

Note: Answers to all practice exercises can be found at the back of the book.

Exercise 11 (Practice)

Identifying Gerunds

Circle all gerunds. Identify which function the gerund is performing in the sentence. Is it the (1) subject of the sentence, (2) direct object (tells *what* after the verb), (3) the noun in a prepositional phrase, or (4) a noun after a linking verb renaming the sentence subject?

1. Relocating our Los Angeles plant is something to consider.

2. We are studying the feasibility of offering in-house seminars in professional communication.

3. Determining the usefulness of the software will take a few days.

4. Winning has always been important to Cheryl.

5. Paula's new job is writing the employee newsletter.

6. Detailing your travel expenses is necessary for full reimbursement.

7. Maintaining good customer relations is an on-going concern of top management.

8. She enjoys writing software.

9. His reporting of the facts was accurate.

10. By flying to New York on Friday, we were able to meet with the client on Saturday.

11. The reason for including these figures is that we want to persuade Mr. Danielson to our position.

12. Purchasing new equipment is something my manager looks forward to.

13. Checking figures before presenting is important for any speech to management.

14. Understanding the client's needs is critical to our success.

15. What are the benefits of following your suggestions?

Exercise 11 (In Class)

Identifying Gerunds

Circle all gerunds. Identify which function the gerund is performing in the sentence. Is it the (1) subject of the sentence, (2) direct object (tells *what* after the verb), (3) the noun in a prepositional phrase, or (4) a noun after a linking verb renaming the sentence subject?

1. Building impressive structures is something this firm does well.

2. Designing wallpaper is Melanie's new job.

3. His traveling to Houston added an additional $1200 to this month's expenses.

4. The responsibility for reimbursing damages rests with either the shipper or your warehouse staff.

5. At the meeting, we discussed Harold's resigning from the project.

6. In discussing the difficulty, Rosemary raised her voice several times.

7. If you have any suggestions for refining this plan, please let me know by Friday.

8. I cannot understand his buying such an expensive printer.

9. Leaving early is not something my manager condones.

10. This plan offers methods for reducing production costs.

11. We can save approximately 10% in office supplies by purchasing in large quantities.

12. Helping others when necessary is what a good team player does.

13. After studying the proposal for several hours, I agreed that it was ready to submit.

14. Suggesting improvements to my manager does not usually please her.

15. Ron suggested a plan for improving security of company documents.

16. We need to develop programs aimed at attracting and retaining qualified employees.

Present Participle

A present participle, besides serving as a noun (called **gerund**), can also serve as an adjective, hence the confusion between the gerund and the present participle as adjective. Their forms are identical—an **-ing** verb not used as a verb—only their function is different.

Since the present participle as adjective modifies or describes the sentence subject, the entire participial phrase can be moved to either side of the subject, and the sentence will sound correct. You cannot move gerund phrases like this.

The present participle (**-ing** ending to verb) can also legitimately be part of the verb in the sentence. But when an **-ing** verb functions *as a verb,* it will have a *to be* form in front of it—*is going, is speaking, will be working, was walking,* etc. If no form of *to be* appears in front, the **-ing** verb form *is not a verb*—it is a **verbal** (either a gerund or present participle as adjective).

If the present participle is serving as an adjective, it will be describing the subject of the sentence; the present participle will **not** describe another word *within the same phrase.*

The following sentences show the **-ing** verb form serving as an **adjective**. **Participial phrases,** as they are called, describe the subject of the sentence.

walking

> **Walking** to work, I noticed the accident.

Walking here is a verbal, not part of the verb. It is functioning as an adjective because *walking to work* describes *I.* The phrase can also be moved to after *I.*

> I, walking to work, noticed the accident.

You can't move gerund phrases around like this. The verb in the sentence is *noticed.*

speaking

> Mr. Garvin, **speaking** to the group of concerned citizens, made his remarks brief.

Speaking is an adjective describing Mr. Garvin. The phrase could also be moved before his name:

> Speaking to the group of concerned citizens, Mr. Garvin made his remarks brief.

The verb in the sentence is *made.* If **speaking** had been a verb in the sentence, a *to be* form would have preceded it.

> Mr. Garvin **will be speaking** this afternoon to the group of concerned citizens.

shopping

David and Jan, **shopping** for a new computer, finally gave up exhausted.

Shopping here is a present participle used as an adjective to describe David and Jan. The entire participial phrase could be moved to the beginning of the sentence (another test for an adjective phrase):

Shopping for a new computer, David and Jan finally gave up exhausted.

The verb in the sentence is *gave up*. Had **shopping** been used as a verb, it would have had a *to be* form in front:

David and Jan were shopping for a new computer when they finally gave up exhausted.

proofreading

Proofreading the manuscript, Donald found 17 errors.

Proofreading is an adjective describing what Donald was doing. It is not the verb in the sentence. The verb in the sentence is *found*. If **Proofreading** had been the verb, **Proofreading** would have been preceded by a *to be* verb form:

Donald was proofreading the manuscript when he found 17 errors.

The participial phrase as adjective could also be moved to appear *after* Donald's name:

Donald, proofreading the manuscript, found 17 errors.

swimming

Swimming to shore, the teams listened over the loudspeaker for the results of the race.

Notice that **swimming** appears first in the sentence, just as a gerund did when it was the the sentence subject. What makes this example an adjective is that the entire phrase *Swimming to shore* describes the subject later on—*teams*. The phrase can also be moved to appear after *teams*:

The teams, swimming to shore, listened over the loudspeaker for the results of the race.

You cannot move gerunds this way. The verb in the sentence is *listened*. Had **swimming** been a verb, it would have been preceded by a *to be* form:

The teams were swimming to shore when they heard over the loudspeaker the results of the race.

Heard is another real verb, but it is the verb in the subordinate clause only.

maintaining

My manager, **maintaining** his self-control, confronted the three violators.

Maintaining here is a present participle used as an adjective to describe *manager*. The phrase could also be moved to appear before manager:

Maintaining his self-control, my manager confronted the three violators.

You cannot move gerunds this way. The verb in the sentence is *confronted*. Had **maintaining** been the verb in the sentence, a *to be* form would have appeared in front:

My manager was maintaining his self-control while he confronted the three violators.

In summary, here are the **-ing** verb forms in their three possible functions: as verb in the sentence, as adjective, and as noun.

Verb   I *was* **walking** to work when I heard the siren.

Adjective   **Walking** *to work*, I noticed the accident.
Noticed is the verb.

Gerund   **Walking** to work is good exercise.
Is is the verb.

Verb   Mr. Garvin *will be* **speaking** this afternoon.

Adjective   Mr. Garvin, **speaking** *to the group of concerned citizens,* made his remarks brief.
Made is the verb.

Gerund   Mr. Garvin enjoys **speaking**.
Direct object—*enjoys what?* The verb is *enjoys*.

Verb   David and Jan *were* **shopping** for a new computer when they finally gave up exhausted.

Adjective   David and Jan, **shopping** *for a new computer,* finally gave up exhausted.
The verb is *gave up*.

Gerund	My favorite activity is **shopping** for a computer. Noun after a linking verb. The verb is *is*—a linking verb.
Verb	Mr. Conway *was* **proofreading** the report for Mr. Jamison.
Adjective	**Proofreading** *the report,* Mr. Conway found several errors. Verb is *found*.
Gerund	**Proofreading** is difficult work. Sentence subject. Verb is *is*—a linking verb here.
Verb	The teams *were* **swimming** to shore when they heard over the loudspeaker the results of the race. *Heard* is the verb of the subordinate clause only.
Adjective	**Swimming** *to shore,* the teams listened over the loudspeaker for the results of the race. Verb is *listened*.
Gerund	I feel refreshed after **swimming**. Noun in prepositional phrase. Verb is *feel*.
Verb	My manager *was* **maintaining** his self-control while he confronted the three violators. *Confronted* is the verb in the subordinate clause only.
Adjective	My manager, **maintaining** *his self-control,* confronted the three violators. Now, *confronted* is the verb of the sentence.
Gerund	My manager is good at **maintaining** self-control when confronting violators. Noun in prepositional phrase—*at maintaining*. Verb is *is*.

Practice and In-Class Exercises

Note: Answers to all practice exercises can be found at the back of the book.

Exercise 12 (Practice)

Identifying Present Participles

Underline present participles being used as a verb (underline both the form of *to be* plus **-ing** action verb) and circle present participles (and their related words) used as adjectives.

If used as an adjective, circle the word the phrase is describing.

1. Ms. Michaels is presenting our findings at the next staff meeting.

2. Arriving at work early, I started answering my mail.

3. Addressing the group, Tim answered everyone's questions.

4. We are sending out flyers announcing our new discount prices.

5. Working rapidly, Joe and Sherry called the entire list of customers.

6. Chris had been speaking for 45 minutes when Ms. Samuel entered the room

7. Standing before a large audience, Dolores presented her evidence brilliantly and without any nervousness.

8. I had been working several hours before I realized that everyone else had gone home.

9. Speaking rapidly, Jeff accused Larry of stealing.

10. Linda will be going to the conference in Los Angeles.

11. Matthew has been preparing our part of the presentation.

12. Running to catch the shuttle bus, I dropped all of the papers.

13. Ron and Ted were operating the new PC's with no problem.

14. Signing the contract, Cliff smiled broadly.

15. Monica is collecting the figures we need for the April report.

Exercise 12 (In Class)
Identifying Present Participles

Underline present participles being used as a verb (underline both the form of *to be* plus **-ing** action verb) and circle present participles (and their related words) used as adjectives. If used as an adjective, circle the word the phrase is describing.

1. Mark will be capturing our ideas in the graphics.

2. Auditing the books, Kevin found several errors.

3. Julie is purchasing two new copy machines for the department.

4. Learning that sales had been good, my manager praised us all.

5. Jeremy, listening intently to the discussion, finally offered some ideas of his own.

6. Because of shortages, the cost of materials is going up.

7. Christine is driving to Boston this week.

8. My supervisor, Ms. Wong, is counting on our participation.

9. The factory has been producing too many defective parts.

10. Raising several good questions, the group waited for answers.

11. The new equipment has been sitting there unused for three weeks.

12. Talking on the telephone, the personnel manager motioned for me to sit down.

13. Low morale has been damaging our productivity since April.

14. Nancy, making her selection, quickly looked to me for approval.

15. The Dallas office, phoning us for information, followed up with three reports for our use.

Past Participle

The past participle is formed from the verb and has an **-ed** ending (for regular verbs). Spelling varies for the **irregulars** like *built*—not *builded* and *known*—not *knowed*.

The past participle can be used in two ways: as part of the verb in the sentence or as an adjective. To function as a verb, the participle *must* be preceded by a *to have* or *to be* verb form: *had known, had written, will have been, has spoken,* etc. Without the *to have* or *to be* form in front, the past participle is an **adjective**, modifying the sentence subject and **is not a verb**.

The following sentences illustrate the past participle as verb, the past participle as adjective, and the present participle as adjective and noun (gerund). You should have no problem telling the difference between the past participle as adjective and the present participle as adjective—they have entirely different endings. The present participle always ends in **-ing**. The past participle usually ends in **-ed**, although irregular endings are common.

Note: Some verbs' simple past tense form and past participle form are identical.

> The audience *asked* several good questions.

Asked is not a past participle here. It is simple past tense. To be a past participle functioning as a verb, the participle must have a *to be*, or *to have* form in front:

> The audience *has asked* several good questions.

Past Participle as Verb

> He **had *written*** the report by noon.

Past Participle as Adj.

> ***Written* by noon**, the report was printed and distributed by 4 p.m.

Pres. Participle as Adj

> ***Writing* the report by noon**, Tim took it to Word Processing for typing.

Present Participle as Noun (Gerund)

> ***Writing* the report by noon** seemed impossible. (sentence subject)

Past Participle as Verb

> My manager **was *driven*** by competition to work 60 hours a week.

Past Participle as Adj.

> ***Driven* by competition to work 60 hours a week**, my manager stayed late again tonight.

Verb is *stayed*.

Pres. Participle as Adj.

    ***Driving* himself to beat the competition,** my manager stayed late again tonight.

Verb is *stayed.*

Pres. Participle as Noun (Gerund)

    My manager enjoys ***driving* himself to beat the competition.**

Direct object telling *what* my manager enjoys. Verb is *enjoys.*

Past Participle as Verb

    This parcel **was *purchased*** when real estate prices were low.

Past Participle as Adj.

    ***Purchased* when real estate prices were low,** this parcel is now worth $400,000.

Verb is *is.*

Present Participle as Adj.

    ***Purchasing* the parcel when real estate prices** were low, Mr. Garvin has now made a sizable profit.

Verb is *has made.*

Present Participle as Noun (Gerund)

    ***Purchasing* the parcel when real estate prices** were low was an excellent idea. (sentence subject)

Verb is *was.*

Perfect Participle

A perfect participle is always used as an adjective and is formed by combining *having* with the past participle.

    Ron, **having *called* on four customers,** quit for the day.

The phrase describes *Ron.*

    Having *completed* the report by 4 p.m., Jennifer took it to her manager for final approval.

The phrase describes *Jennifer.*

    Having *located* the files, Mr. Myers began his research.

The phrase describes *Mr. Myers.*

    Ann discovered the error, **having *looked* through six pages of figures.**

The phrase describes *Ann.*

Practice and In-Class Exercises

Note: Answers to all practice exercises can be found at the back of the book.

EXERCISE 13 (Practice)
Identifying Past Participles

Underline with two lines past participles used as a verb (underline both the form of *to be* or *to have* plus the **-ed** action verb), and circle past participles used as adjectives. If the participle serves as an adjective, draw an arrow to the word outside the phrase the adjective modifies. Some sentences contain no past participles.

1. The entrance to the building was blocked by snow.

2. Cheryl has taken the equipment to the repair shop.

3. The team members have consistently mentioned several worthwhile considerations.

4. Received early this morning, the shipment was left on the receiving dock.

5. I had accomplished five important tasks by noon.

6. Driven by the desire to succeed, Margaret did as much as she could to gain visibility in her job.

7. Mr. Wilson had predicted that we would have several problems with the project.

8. The report typed by Katherine will be ready for duplication by 2 p.m. tomorrow.

9. By Thursday, we had concluded our study.

10. The profits and losses were shared equally by all.

11. The conference announcements have been mailed.

12. Completed at today's meeting, our suggestions were forwarded to Personnel.

13. The 17 pages that we had recently completed needed a lot of revising.

14. We shipped your order yesterday.

15. Used by everyone in the department, the new computer needed repairs within three months.

16. The project has been delayed because of revisions requested by the customer.

Exercise 13 (In Class)
Identifying Past Participles

Underline with two lines past participles used as a verb (underline both the form of *to be* or *to have* plus the **-ed** action verb), and circle past participles used as adjectives. If the participle serves as an adjective, draw an arrow to the word outside the phrase the adjective modifies. Some sentences contain not past participles.

1. Based on this information, we have decided to extend credit.

2. The same comment was restated by Mr. Cervantes.

3. The project has gone over budget by $5,000.

4. That was a comment spoken with confidence.

5. The shipment remained on the dock for two days.

6. This equipment was purchased when prices were lower.

7. He accurately predicted sales for the last three quarters.

8. Researched hastily, the report had several serious flaws.

9. The legal documents removed from the vault were carefully guarded.

10. This fabric, manufactured of flame-resistant material, costs us $6.00 a yard to produce.

Exercise 14 (Practice)
Identifying Participles and Gerunds

In the following sentences, circle present or past participles used as adjectives and mark accordingly. Underline with a double line present and past participles functioning as part of the verb. Underline with one line gerunds used as nouns.

1. The raw materials were supplied by our Pittsburgh plant.

2. Writing a long report is a difficult task.

3. He has created problems with most, if not all, of our clients.

4. Instructions were given to leave the figures on Ms. Litton's desk.

5. Working without a break, we soon completed the report.

6. Before ordering the new laser printer, you need to ask Richard whether we can afford it.

7. Walking to the office, he passed a construction site.

8. The woman speaking to the new hires is Mary Ramirez.

9. Hoping that he would be invited to speak at the meeting, Brett prepared several things to say.

10. I am suggesting Mallorie for the promotion because she has the qualifications.

11. The following furniture was ordered: three tables, three desks, four chairs, and four sofas.

12. William, working as fast as possible, hoped to finish the graphics for the afternoon staff meeting.

13. After listening to the news broadcast, we went back to work.

14. Always suggesting simplistic solutions, David never seemed to impress his manager.

15. Angered by the lack of progress in contract negotiations, the union members threatened to strike.

Exercise 14 (In Class)
Identifying Participles and Gerunds

In the following sentences, circle present or past participles used as adjectives and mark accordingly. Underline with a double line present and past participles functioning as part of the verb. Underline with one line gerunds used as nouns.

1. Marcella has relocated to the new Houston office.

2. The person speaking with her is Sandra Baines, Vice-president of Marketing.

3. Sharla, changing her mind, submitted an application for the position.

4. Sales territories have been expanded to make better use of sales personnel.

5. The memos lying on the desk are ready for distribution.

6. He has not been spending the necessary time to do the work right.

7. Planning to keep the announcement a secret, Bob asked that I tell no one.

8. Mr. Morgan, finished with his work, left for the day.

9. Reaching the proper target market is critical if we are to be successful.

10. Marsha Jones, successfully completing the requirements, was hired on March 23.

11. The advertising campaign developed by Roberta Kleinmann has been submitted for final approval.

12. Finding Building 3 took longer than we expected.

13. We have purchased new carpets and furniture for the office.

14. Margarita, wanting to confirm her suspicions of a company takeover, listened intently outside the door.

15. We must pay hourly employees for working overtime.

16. The photocopy machine located in the break room is not designed for the volume of copies made each month.

17. We may be able to reduce costs by centralizing our distribution system.

IDENTIFYING SUBJECT AND VERB

This section is, perhaps, the most important part of the text for this reason: in order for you to use grammar correctly and punctuate accurately (the goals of this book), you must first be able to identify the subject and verb of the sentence.

For example, one aspect of using grammar correctly is what's called *subject/verb agreement*: if the subject is in a singular form (*he*), the verb must also be in a singular form (*is*). Although the subject is easy to pick out in most cases, in more difficult sentences, it takes some knowledge of grammar to see the true subject. In these cases, with little or no understanding of grammatical structures, it is easy to pick the wrong noun. Thinking a plural noun to be the subject, one would then make the verb plural as well. Your reader, seeing the true [singular] subject, would see your use of a plural verb with it. This *mismatch* is improper grammar and often jolts the reader to see such errors.

Being able to correctly identify the subject and verb of the sentences is also essential to using punctuation marks correctly. Through the proper or improper use of punctuation, you subtly convey to the reader your understanding of English. Punctuation errors discovered by the reader, too, jolt him/her and often interrupt the reader's train of thought.

Isolating the subject and verb is not as easy as one might think. Yet, most grammar texts assume that students can easily identify the subject and verb of the sentence once the definitions of **noun** and **verb** have been introduced. Unfortunately, this superficial level of presentation works only with sentence examples that are extremely short and simple.

As soon as students are presented with real-world sentences, often 10-20+ words long, students become quickly confused and unable in most cases to find the subject and verb. The reason for this difficulty is that most real-world sentences contain elements that look like subjects and verbs but aren't (i.e., verbals, nouns in prepositional phrases, and direct objects).

Since subject/verb isolation is more complex than it first appears, your mastering of all of the previous material in the text was necessary groundwork for this section— developing the ability to identify the subject and verb of real-world sentences. The process of subject/verb identification you are about to learn, and which will work for a sentence of any length, is what could be called a *process of elimination* approach.

You will now use the material you have learned about parts of speech and verbals to rule out the words that cannot be the subject and verb in the sentence. For this method to work successfully, you must have a clear understanding of the concepts presented thus far in the text. Although this approach may seem to be very time-consuming at first, with practice you should be able to apply these steps very rapidly.

PROCESS OF ELIMINATION
APPROACH TO ISOLATING SUBJECT AND VERB

To accurately isolate the subject and verb of any sentence, apply the following steps in this order to the sentence:

1. Cross out any subordinate clauses (adverb, adjective, or noun types). These clauses have their own subject and verb, but they have nothing to do with the main clause subject and verb.

2. From the words remaining, cross out all participial phrases (past or present participles and related words that form a phrase being used as an adjective).

3. Cross out all prepositional phrases in the remaining words. These phrases do not contain a verb, but they always contain a noun. This noun can be confusing and cause you to think it is the subject of the main clause. The noun in a prepositional phrase **will never be** the subject of the main clause.

4. From the words remaining, cross out all infinitives plus any words that go with it. An infinitive will never be the verb in the sentence. A word of caution: occasionally the infinitive will be the sentence subject. If you complete this seven-step process and find you have no sentence subject, or the remaining noun makes no sense with the verb, the re- maining word is a direct object and not the subject. Look back to see if you crossed out an infinitive. If you did, put the infinitive back in as the sentence subject. If the infinitive makes no sense as the subject, the subject is *you* understood.

5. Cross out all adjectives.

6. Cross out all adverbs.

7. Cross out all coordinating conjunctions.

Once you have crossed out all seven types of constructions and parts of speech where the subject and verb cannot be, you are left with only a few words to choose from.

The only words we have not removed are nouns and verbs (plus helping verbs like *does, do, did, should, could,* etc.).

When two nouns remain, one will be the sentence subject and the other a direct object telling *what*. If you're not sure which one is the sentence subject, try each noun with the verb remaining. Normally, only one of the two nouns will make logical sense. If they both sound logical with the verb, look back to the original sentence and determine the subject from the meaning intended.

Several examples follow which show how to isolate the subject and verb using the step-by-step process just described:

> Joe quickly wrote the memo in his office before he went to an important meeting.
> 1. Cross out all subordinate clauses—adverb, adjective, or noun—*before he went to an important meeting*—subordinate clause, adverb type.

> Joe quickly wrote the memo in his office....
> 2. Cross out all participial phrases serving as adjectives—none
> 3. Cross out all prepositional phrases from the remaining words—*in his office*

> Joe quickly wrote the memo....
> 4. Cross out all infinitive phrases—none
> 5. Cross out all adjectives—*the*

> Joe quickly wrote...memo....
> 6. Cross out all adverbs—*quickly* (tells how)

> Joe...wrote...memo....
> 7. Cross out all coordinating conjunctions—none

You are left with three words—two nouns and a simple past tense verb. *Wrote* is obviously the verb of the main clause. What is the subject? Memo or Joe? If you're not sure, try each one with the verb: is it *Joe wrote* or *Memo wrote?* Obviously, *Memo wrote* makes no sense, so the subject here is *Joe* and the verb is *wrote*. *Memo* is a direct object telling *what* Joe wrote.

> The recent order which we recently received from the manufacturer was shipped to you yesterday.
> 1. Cross out all subordinate clauses—adverb, adjective, or noun—*which we recently received from the manufacturer*—subordinate clause, adjective type, tells which one? which order?

> The recent order...was shipped to you yesterday.
> 2. Cross out all participial phrases serving as adjectives—none
> 3. Cross out all prepositional phrases from the remaining words—*to you*

> The recent order...was shipped...yesterday.
> 4. Cross out all infinitive phrases—none
> 5. Cross out all adjectives—*The, recent*

...order...was shipped...yesterday

    6. Cross out all adverbs—*yesterday* (tells when)

...order...was shipped....

    7. Cross out all coordinating conjunctions—none

You are left with only the subject *order* and verb *was shipped*. In this case, you have a *verb phrase—was* must be included as part of the verb.

Although Steve and the accountant worked hard to finish the report by noon, it was not completed by the deadline.

    1. Cross out all subordinate clauses—adverb, adjective, or noun—*Although Steve and the accountant worked hard to finish the report by noon*—subordinate clause, adverb type.

...it was not completed by the deadline.

    2. Cross out all participial phrases serving as adjectives—none
    3. Cross out all prepositional phrases from the remaining words—*by the deadline*

...it was not completed....

    4. Cross out all infinitive phrases—none
    5. Cross out all adjectives—none
    6. Cross out all adverbs—*not*

...it was...completed....

Obviously removing *not* changes the meaning of the sentence drastically, but we're not looking for meaning here, only parts of speech where the subject and verb cannot be found.

    7. Cross out all coordinating conjunctions—none

You are left with the subject *it* and verb *was completed*.

Reviewing all of the options available to the employees, Ms. Morris has recommended that they take additional courses.

    1. Cross out all subordinate clauses—adverb, adjective, or noun—*that they take additional courses.* (subordinate clause, noun type, telling *what* Ms. Morris has recommended)

Reviewing all of the options available to the employees, Ms. Morris has recommended....

    2. Cross out all participial phrases serving as adjectives—*Reviewing all of the options available to the employees* serves as an adjective modifying Ms. Morris.

...Ms. Morris has recommended....

3. Cross out all prepositional phrases from the remaining words—none
4. Cross out all infinitive phrases—none
5. Cross out all adjectives—none
6. Cross out all adverbs—none
7. Cross out all coordinating conjunctions—none

You are left with the subject *Ms. Morris* and verb phrase *has recommended*.

In the company directory advertisement, you will find a list of our company's services.

1. Cross out all subordinate clauses—adverb, adjective, or noun—none
2. Cross out all participial phrases serving as adjectives—none
3. Cross out all prepositional phrases from the remaining words—*in the company directory advertisement* and *of our company's services*

...you will find a list....

4. Cross out all infinitive phrases—none
5. Cross out all adjectives—*a*

...you will find...list....

6. Cross out all adverbs—none
7. Cross out all coordinating conjunctions—none

You are left with two nouns, *you* and *list,* and one verb phrase, *will find*. Which is the correct subject, *you* or *list?* Try each with the verb—is it *List will find* or *You will find? You will find* makes more sense, so *list* is the direct object telling what *you* will find.

Our sales representatives report that the public is responding enthusiastically to the new X4300 copier.

1. Cross out all subordinate clauses—adverb, adjective, or noun—*that the public is responding enthusiastically to the new X4300 copier*—subordinate clause, noun type, telling *what* the representatives report.

Our sales representatives report....

2. Cross out all participial phrases serving as adjectives—none
3. Cross out all prepositional phrases from the remaining words—none
4. Cross out all infinitive phrases—none
5. Cross out all adjectives—*our* and *sales*

...representatives report....

6. Cross out all adverbs—none
7. Cross out all coordinating conjunctions—none

You are left with the subject *representatives* and verb *report*.

The supplies can be obtained immediately at Johnson's Office Supplies, or they can be ordered at a lower price from Taylor's.

1. Cross out all subordinate clauses—adverb, adjective, or noun—none
2. Cross out all participial phrases serving as adjectives—none
3. Cross out all prepositional phrases from the remaining words—*at Johnson's Office Supplies, at a lower price, from Taylor's*

The supplies can be obtained immediately..., or they can be ordered....

4. Cross out all infinitive phrases—none
5. Cross out all adjectives—*The*

...supplies can be obtained immediately..., or they can be ordered....

6. Cross out all adverbs—*immediately*

...supplies can be obtained..., or they can be ordered....

7. Cross out all coordinating conjunctions—*or*

...supplies can be obtained...they can be ordered....

You are left with several words here. This is an example of a compound sentence—two independent clauses of equal weight—one is not subordinate to the other. How do you know one is not subordinate to the other? Neither one begins with a subordinate word such as *although, since, that, which.*

Independent Clause #1: *supplies* (subject) and *can be obtained* (verb); Independent Clause #2: *they* (subject) and *can be ordered* (verb). In this example, since you don't have a main clause and a subordinate clause, it is more correct to say you have *two independent clauses,* rather than *two main clauses.*

Tom, who is Ms. Thompson's assistant, readily agreed.

1. Cross out all subordinate clauses—adverb, adjective, or noun—*who is Ms. Thompson's assistant*—subordinate clause, adjective type, describing *Tom.*

Tom...readily agreed.

2. Cross out all participial phrases serving as adjectives—none
3. Cross out all prepositional phrases from the remaining words—none
4. Cross out all infinitive phrases—none
5. Cross out all adjectives—none
6. Cross out all adverbs—*readily* (tells when)

Tom...agreed.

7. Cross out all coordinating conjunctions—none

You are left with the subject *Tom* and verb *agreed.*

Before you purchase a car, first check the recommendations of any consumer guide.

1. Cross out all subordinate clauses—adverb, adjective, or noun—*before you purchase a car*—subordinate clause, adverb type, telling *when*.

...first check the recommendations of any consumer guide.

2. Cross out all participial phrases serving as adjectives—none
3. Cross out all prepositional phrases from the remaining words—*of any consumer guide*

...first check the recommendations....

4. Cross out all infinitive phrases—none
5. Cross out all adjectives—*the*

...first check...recommendations....

6. Cross out all adverbs—*first* (tells when)

...check...recommendations....

7. Cross out all coordinating conjunctions—none

You are left with two words, a noun and verb. Which one is the verb? *check*—denotes action in this sentence. Now put the remaining noun with it—is it *recommendations check?* That combination makes no sense. Who should check? *You* understood. This sentence illustrates the *command form* in English. The *you* isn't printed, but it's understood to be the subject. *Recommendations* is **not** the subject here, then, but the direct object, telling *what* you should check. The subject of the sentence is *you* understood. *You check.* That combination makes sense.

I might not have realized that point if it hadn't been for my manager's counsel.

1. Cross out all subordinate clauses—adverb, adjective, or noun—*if it hadn't been for my manager's counsel*—subordinate clause, adverb type

I might not have realized that point....

2. Cross out all participial phrases serving as adjectives—none
3. Cross out all prepositional phrases from the remaining words—none
4. Cross out all infinitive phrases—none
5. Cross out all adjectives—*that*

I might not have realized...point....

6. Cross out all adverbs—*not*

I might...have realized point....

7. Cross out all coordinating conjunctions—none

You are left with two nouns, *I* and *point,* and one verb phrase—*might have realized.* Which noun is the subject here—*I* or *point?* Is it *I might have realized* or *Point might have realized?* Obviously, it's *I might have realized. Point* here is the direct object, telling *what* I might not have realized.

Although I may not get the promotion, to want it is not a sin.
1. Cross out all subordinate clauses—adverb, adjective, or noun—*Although I may not get the promotion*—subordinate clause, adverb type.

...to want it is not a sin....
2. Cross out all participial phrases serving as adjectives—none
3. Cross out all prepositional phrases from the remaining words—none
4. Cross out all infinitive phrases—*to want it*

...is not a sin....
5. Cross out all adjectives—*a*

...is not...sin....
6. Cross out all adverbs—*not*

...is...sin....
7. Cross out all coordinating conjunctions—none

You are left with two words—a noun *sin* and verb *is.* Putting the two together, is it *sin is?* If you re-read the sentence, you will find that *sin is* is not at all the meaning here. Is the subject *you* understood? *You is?* This can't be right—or it would be *you are.* This is a case where the infinitive should not have been removed—*to want* is the sentence subject—in fact, you could say the entire infinitive phrase is the sentence subject—*to want it* and the verb is *is. Sin* here is a direct object telling *what* it is not.

Lois wanted to lead the discussion.
1. Cross out all subordinate clauses—adverb, adjective, or noun—none
2. Cross out all participial phrases serving as adjectives—none
3. Cross out all prepositional phrases from the remaining words—none
4. Cross out all infinitive phrases—*to lead the discussion*

Lois wanted....
5. Cross out all adjectives—none
6. Cross out all adverbs—none
7. Cross out all coordinating conjunctions—none

You are left with the subject *Lois* and the verb *wanted.*

The woman I trained is now manager of the Personnel Department.

1. Cross out all subordinate clauses—adverb, adjective, or noun—*I trained*—subordinate clause, adjective type. Remember that some adjective clauses are missing the introductory *that*. Mentally replace the *that* to find *hidden* adjective clauses.

The woman...is now manager of the Personnel Department.

2. Cross out all participial phrases serving as adjectives—none

The woman...is now manager of the Personnel Department.

3. Cross out all prepositional phrases from the remaining words—*of the Personnel Department*

The woman...is now manager....

4. Cross out all infinitive phrases—none

The woman...is now manager....

5. Cross out all adjectives—*the*

...woman...is now manager....

6. Cross out all adverbs—*now*

...woman...is...manager....

7. Cross out all coordinating conjunctions—none

...woman...is...manager....

You are left with two nouns, *woman* and *manager*, and the verb *is*. It should be obvious from the order of the three remaining words that *is* is a linking verb here, linking the first noun to the second—linking the subject to a word that renames the subject. A linking verb can also link a noun to an adjective, a word that describes the subject. But in this case, *is* is followed by a noun. So the subject is *woman* and the verb is *is*.

Practice and In-Class Exercises

Note: Answers to all practice exercises can be found at the back of the book.

Exercise 15 (Practice)
Identifying Subject and Verb

Underline the independent clause subject with one line and the independent clause verb (or verb phrase) with two lines.

1. Mr. Gordon, who has responsibility in this case, will make the final decision.

2. Our new department manager, planning to make major changes, first fired two secretaries for excessive tardiness.

3. Factors that managers may want to consider in determining an employee's contribution and corresponding performance rating are (1) level of individual performance, (2) length of time since last increase, and (3) position in salary range.

4. Each person who has enrolled in the course will get time off to attend class.

5. As soon as we receive your completed application form, we can process your request.

6. Get feedback from supervisors as well as trainees.

7. His argument in favor of the proposal did not impress my manager.

8. Even if we can produce 5,000 more units by next week, we still cannot guarantee a profit this month.

9. Why are we losing money?

10. I believe, Ms. Edmunds, that the contract will protect us on this issue.

11. Our last investment, suggested by Tom Roberts, was very successful.

12. Our profits have declined this year despite attempts to increase sales.

13. The supervisor will change next week's schedule if it is needed.

14. We hope that Gina will attend the presentation on February 9 or send a substitute.

15. Tom will finish the project himself or will arrange for someone else to finish it.

16. No problems are expected in meeting the planned completion dates.

17. All supervisors on the third floor endorse the purchase of an additional photocopy machine.

18. By automating now, we will create a system that will hold down future salary costs and, at the same time, increase our capacity for fast turnaround and response to customers.

19. For more detail of the proposed training program, refer to Appendix D.

Exercise 15 (In Class)
Identifying Subject and Verb

Underline the independent clause subject with one line and the independent clause verb (or verb phrase) with two lines.

1. Janet has been promoted three times and is now eligible for another raise.

2. We have checked our records and find that you are correct.

3. Why has our new filing system caused so much confusion?

4. When four more members arrive, we can start the meeting.

5. Compensation is a major element of cost and has a significant influence on employee productivity.

6. Mr. Elliott began his remarks when only two people were present.

7. Because her report contained several errors, Kelly did not get the promotion.

8. As I was walking to the lunch room, I noticed my manager speaking with Mr. Brooks.

9. Until the company develops a new hiring policy, it will attract few new hires.

10. Because I disagreed with Lynn's idea, I could not support a change in managers.

11. How many representatives are we planning to send to Cincinnati for the May convention?

12. Jack is phoning Mr. Randall now to discuss the merger.

13. We intend to purchase three new printers despite our budget difficulties.

14. Mr.Clark has been more productive since Diane assumed several of his routine responsibilities.

15. Reviewing all of the resumes that were submitted, I called Personnel about three of the candidates.

16. As the attached worksheet reveals, the cost of inconvenience and delay is conservatively estimated at $13,500 per year.

17. Recovery of the company's investment in an automated system will occur in approximately two years from the date the new system becomes operational.

18. All managers interviewed about the new proposal agree that efficiency will improve over the next three years.

19. Mr. Kawahara also stated that replacement costs are approximately $50,000.

SUBJECT/VERB AGREEMENT

What we have been working toward so far is gaining enough knowledge about sentence structure to be able to use proper *subject-verb agreement* when we write. *Agreement* means that the subject and verb should agree *in number*. When the subject is singular, *Barbara,* the verb should also be in a singular form, *studies*. It would sound very wrong to say, *Barbara study* (the plural form and form used with *I*).

Most of our application of this concept called *agreement* comes easily, particularly if English is our native language. Where we sometimes have trouble, however, is when we have selected the wrong word as the subject of the sentence—thinking the subject is plural—we then mistakenly make our verb plural to match it.

Subject/Verb agreement problems are more likely to occur when the sentence contains (1) a prepositional phrase between the subject and verb and/or (2) a singular form indefinite pronoun subject. When determining the sentence subject, ignore the prepositional phrase.

Also remember that certain indefinite pronouns are **always** singular—*each, either, neither, one, everyone,* and *everybody*.

Each of her reports **is** accurate.

Each of the members **is required** to be present.

Neither of her mistakes **is** significant.

The contract between the employer and employees **was signed** yesterday.

One of our managers **came** to us from the east coast.

Every **one** of our terminals **has been repaired.**

The **price** of new cars **has been increasing** lately.

A huge trade **gap** with foreign countries **persists.**

Subject/Verb agreement can also be difficult when the sentence is in the form of a question. Questions invert our normal word order and so make it more difficult to quickly tell what the subject is and whether it needs a singular or plural verb.

Has/Have their profits increased this year?

To determine the proper form of the helping verb, answer the question, which will put the words in their normal order:

Their profits **have** increased this year.

Now it is easy to see that *profits* (a plural form) is the subject of the sentence; therefore, we need the plural form of *to have* to go with the verb *increased*.

Another subject/verb agreement problem occurs with the two constructions: *A number of* .... and *The number of*.... The rule is, *A number of*.... requires a **singular** verb. *The number of*.... requires a **plural** verb.

A number of complaints **were** registered.

The entire verb phrase is *were registered*.

The number of complaints **is** small.

A number of people **have** already arrived.

The entire verb phrase is *have arrived*.

The number of people who have already arrived **is** small.

Notice that the noun following *of* in all cases is plural. Ignore this word and look instead at whether you are dealing with *a number of* or *the number of*.

Practice and In-Class Exercises

Note: Answers to all practice exercises can be found at the back of the book.

Exercise 16 (Practice)
Subject/Verb Agreement

Select the correct form of the verb in each sentence.

1. What books (has/have) Miss Jennings recommended lately?

2. Neither of her mistakes (is/are) significant.

3. The recommendation of the managers (is/are) that we begin production immediately.

4. The new assistant with five excellent recommendations (is/are) being considered for Mr. Statler's replacement.

5. All of these suggested changes (was/were) made by Mr. Ellis.

6. Either of the two books (has/have) the answer.

7. Langley, Brown, and Smithson (has/have) just been given the contract to build our new suite of offices. (one firm)

8. We believe that the cost of maintenance and supplies for our computer printers (is/are) greater than the cost for typewriter maintenance and supplies.

9. Consumer perception of quality and value (is/are) strongly linked with brand name recognition.

Exercise 16 (In Class)
Subject/Verb Agreement

Select the correct form of the verb in each sentence.

1. There (is/are) a number of questions to be answered.

2. Economics (is/are) among the required courses for business majors.

3. A review of the budget figures (reveal/reveals) no obvious flaws.

4. The invoice for the last three shipments (has/have) been lost.

5. Confusion about policy statements, vacation schedules, and performance appraisals (creates/create) a sense of urgency.

6. Every one of the new components (is/are) defective.

7. Anderson, Jones, and Stratton (has/have) introduced a new insulating material. (the name of one firm)

8. The choice of doctors and hospitals (is/are) limited with this health plan.

9. The reason for the recommendations (is/are) that Mr. Shapiro asked for my suggestions.

10. The purposes of these reports (is/are) to analyze the causes of the continued unfavorable variances in printing expenses and to bring the budget back into line.

PRONOUN USAGE

PRONOUN/ANTECEDENT AGREEMENT

Sentence subjects must also *agree* with any pronouns used later in the sentence that refer back to the subject. When the subject is singular, the pronouns later used to refer to the singular subject must also be singular.

People's names and many nouns are easy to see as singular:

Nancy should bring **her** notes to the meeting.

My manager will likely get the promotion **he** hopes for.

Although I disagree, **Don** has a right to **his** opinion.

More difficult to use correctly are the *indefinite pronouns—neither, everybody, everyone, nobody, each, everyone, etc.*

These are all **singular** and, when referred to again in the sentence, need **singular** pronouns to go with them:

neither	his/her
everybody	his/her
everyone	his/her
nobody	his/her
each	his/her
every	his/her

Each **person** should bring **his or her** copy of the report to the meeting.

Each **executive** must keep **his or her** own notes.

Every **employee** may pick up **his or her** paycheck at Barbara's desk after 9 a.m. on Friday.

Everyone should report to **his or her** work station by 7:30 a.m.

Neither of the managers admitted **his** real feelings about the issue. (if both managers are male)

Neither of the managers admitted **his or her** real feelings about the issue. (if one manager is male and the other female)

Somebody left **his or her** calculator in the conference room.

Nobody wants to risk **his or her** reputation over this issue.

Each of our competitors has reduced **its** prices.

Everyone should complete **his or her** part of the report before closing today.

In cases with *each, every,* and *everyone,* you can often change the subject to plural to avoid the his/her construction:

All executives must keep **their** own notes.

All employees may pick up **their** paychecks at Barbara's desk after 9 a.m. on Friday.

All employees should report to **their** workstations by 7:30 a.m.

All of our competitors have reduced **their** prices.

All involved should complete **their** part of the report before closing today.

In summary, some singular pronoun situations can be turned into plural by using *all* instead. This construction is easier because *all* requires the plural pronoun to go with it. In English, the plural pronoun *their* is neither masculine nor feminine.

Practice and In-Class Exercises

Note: Answers to all practice exercises can be found at the back of the book.

Exercise 17 (Practice)
Pronoun/Antecedent Agreement

Circle the correct pronoun form that matches **in number** the noun it refers to (singular with singular, plural with plural).

1. A person can usually improve if (they/he,she) wants to.

2. When a customer expresses (their/his,her) dissatisfaction, we should listen courteously.

3. Everyone should write (their/his,her) name on each page of the application form.

4. Each manager must use (their/his,her) own funds for office improvements.

5. Each person must make (their/his,her) own decision on the matter.

6. All of us should bring (our/his,her) ideas to the meeting.

7. Every woman in this office needs (their/her) own phone.

8. Each new employee should promptly obtain (their/his,her) identification card from personnel.

9. Everyone who enters the building after normal working hours must show the guard (their/his,her) ID badge.

10. Everybody wants (their/his,her) share of praise.

Exercise 17 (In Class)
Pronoun/Antecedent Agreement

Circle the correct pronoun form that matches **in number** the noun it refers to (singular with singular, plural with plural).

1. It is a wise manager who understands (their/his,her) employees.

2. One of them paid (their/his,her) tuition late.

3. Many of the employees did (their/his,her) best.

4. Everyone had to move (their/his,her) car when the announcement was made that the parking lot was being repaved.

5. All vendors should send (their/his,her) invoices directly to Accounting.

6. The corporation reports that (their/its) earnings for this year are improving.

7. No man or woman should overlook the possibilities for (their/his, her) advancement within this company.

8. All salespeople must sign (their/his,her) report.

9. Every employee will receive (their/his,her) paycheck today.

10. All of the staff must do (their/his,her) share to make the party a success.

PRONOUNS AS SUBJECTS AND OBJECTS

When the pronoun serves as the subject of the sentence, or as one of two or three subjects (compound subject), use what's called the *subject form* of the pronoun. When the pronoun falls in a prepositional phrase (as the noun at the end) or is in a *direct object* position, use the *object form*.

Singular		Plural	
Subject Form	Object Form	Subject Form	Object Form
I	me	we	us
you	you	you	you
he	him	they	them
she	her	they	them
it	it	they	them
who	whom	who	whom

> Give the report to Barbara or **me.**

The object form, **me**, is required here because the pronoun occurs in a prepositional phrase beginning with *to,* a preposition. Another test is to temporarily remove *Barbara or* and read the sentence again.

> Give the report to—I? or me?

Often, taking out the other noun or pronoun and the coordinating conjunction will help your ear to *hear* the right answer.

> Between you and **me,** that idea won't work.

The object form **me** is required here because the pronoun occurs in a prepositional phrase beginning with the preposition *between.*

> Michael and **she** could work on the presentation together.

The pronoun in question here is in a subject position, *Michael* being the other subject. If in doubt, remove the other subject and coordinating conjunction and begin the sentence with the pronoun in question. Temporarily removing the other words will help your ear *hear* the proper answer.

> **Her** could work on the presentation?
> or
> **She** could work on the presentation?

Obviously, **she** is the correct answer here.

The $5,000 reward should be divided between Donna and **me.**

This sentence is another prepositional phrase situation—*between* is a preposition, so the object form is required.

The sales manager doesn't want Bill and **me** to work together.

The pronoun here is in the *direct object* position, telling *what* the sales manager doesn't want. If you don't easily recognize the direct object, remove the other noun or pronoun and the coordinating conjunction to help your ear *hear* the right answer:

The sales manager doesn't want I to work...?

or

The sales manager doesn't want me to work...?

Obviously, *I* sounds incorrect here.

Everyone except Dr. Marshall and **him** will be at the meeting.

Except is a preposition, so the object form is required. If you didn't know that *except* was a preposition, remove the other noun in the prepositional phrase and the coordinating conjunction to help your ear *hear* the right answer.

Everyone except he will be at the meeting?

or

Everyone except him will be at the meeting?

Obviously, the object form *him* is the correct choice here.

Ken gave Sandra and **me** the blueprints.

The pronoun here is actually in a prepositional phrase, although the preposition is not printed. What did Ken give? The direct object is *blueprints*. If you were to change the structure and put the direct object after the verb, the sentence would read, *Ken gave the blueprints to Sandra and me.* Really, then, *Sandra and me* is in a prepositional phrase, although the preposition is not printed.

An easier way to determine the correct pronoun form here is to temporarily remove *Sandra and* to help your ear *hear* the right answer:

Ken gave me the blueprints?
or
Ken gave I the blueprints?

Obviously, the object form is the right one. (Technically, *Sandra* and *me* are called *indirect objects* here.)

Chris asked both you and **us** to speak to her.

This pronoun is another *direct object* type. To help your ear get the correct pronoun form, temporarily remove *both you and* and re-read the sentence.

Is it

Chris asked **us** to speak to her?
or
Chris asked **we** to speak to her?

Obviously, **us** is the right one.

Mr. Harrison saw you and **her** arrive late.

The pronouns here are in *direct object* position, telling what Mr. Harrison saw. If you weren't sure which form to use, temporarily remove *you and* and re-read the sentence. Is it

Mr. Harrison saw **she** arrive late?
or
Mr. Harrison saw **her** arrive late?

Her is the correct choice.

Practice and In-Class Exercises

Note: Answers to all practice exercises can be found at the back of the book.

Exercise 18 (Practice)

Pronoun Forms as Subjects and Objects

Select the correct pronoun form for each sentence that follows.

1. Give the report to either Bonnie or (I, me, myself).

2. Elaine and (I, me, myself) are planning to attend the banquet together.

3. I spoke with (she, her) and (he, him) about the new policies.

4. Carl, Betty, and (she, her) listened intently to the new marketing executive.

5. The manager arrived with Ms. Davis and (he, him).

6. The proposal written by Alex and (she, her) stands a very good chance of being accepted.

7. They seated Mark between Sally and (I, me, myself).

8. I received a worthwhile report from (she, her) and Mrs. Rizzo.

9. (He, him) and Rosa walked with Greg and (I, me, myself) to the cafeteria.

10. She, her manager, and (I, me, myself) discussed the production problems at great length.

Exercise 18 (In Class)

Pronoun Forms as Subjects and Objects

Select the correct pronoun form for each sentence that follows.

1. Let Roy and (I, me, myself) discuss the new procedures.

2. Tina and (she, her) have worked together for five years.

3. The bus driver watched Cathy and (he, him) get off the bus.

4. The report from Mr. Pierce and (she, her) arrived today.

5. Just between you and (I, me, myself), I think John will get the promotion.

6. Ask Gerry and (I, me, myself) for any equipment you need.

7. The customer set up the conference call with Barry and (I, me, myself) to discuss the change in schedule.

8. Your marketing representative can arrange for Margaret or (I, me, myself) to contact you before Thursday.

9. By phoning the office or (I, me, myself) personally, you can get the help you need.

10. He asked that they write to Dave Jamison or (I, me, myself) about the distribution problem.

WHO/WHOM

One of the most difficult grammatical rules deals with the use of *who/whom*. Learning which to use is easier if you understand that *who* or *whom* can function in four ways:

- as subject of an independent or subordinate clause
- as object in an independent clause or subordinate clause
- as object in a prepositional phrase
- after a linking verb, renaming the subject

*When you can substitute **I, she, he, we,** or **they,** use **who**.* These are *subject* forms. *When you can substitute **me, her, him, us,** or **them,** use **whom**.* These are **object** forms.

Who as Subject of Independent Clause

Whenever the word is the subject of an independent clause, the proper form will always be *who*.

Who came in late?

Answer the question by substituting another pronoun here—your *ear* will tell you which pronoun makes sense. Our ear tells us that *Her came in late* is wrong. We know to say, *She came in late.* Remember the rule—when you would use *she,* the correct pronoun is *who.*

Who stayed to clean the lunchroom?

He stayed to clean the lunchroom.

Who as Subject of an Adjective Clause

Who often appears in an adjective clause as the subject of the clause:

He is the man **who keeps the best files** on that company.

He keeps the best files

Jim, **who types accurately and carefully**, was hired last week.

He types accurately and carefully

My manager, **who was born in Minneapolis**, moved to California when he was 10.

She was born in Minneapolis

David, **who wrote only two chapters of the report**, was credited with writing all of it.

He wrote only two chapters of the report.

Anyone **who would like a copy of the report** should send me a note.

He/she would like a copy of the report.

Who as Subject of a Noun Clause

Who/Whom do you think is the best programmer?

In answering the question, the structure reveals that this is a noun clause:

I think (that) she is the best programmer.
I think...**she** is the best programmer.

Either form is grammatically correct, but you must insert the *that* at least temporarily to properly analyze the grammatical construction. When *that* is inserted, it becomes obvious that the pronoun is the subject of a noun clause which answers the question, what? I think what? *That* is a subordinate conjunction here, and the subject of the noun clause is the pronoun, so the subject form *who* is required.

Whom as Object in an Independent Clause

Whom did you hire to fill the position?

When the question is answered, the object function appears more obvious:

I hired *her* to fill the position.

Whom as Object in an Adjective Clause

When the adjective clause already has a subject, *whom* is the correct choice—it will now be performing an object function:

He is the individual **whom we respect the most**.

We respect *him* the most.

Liz Sheppard, **whom we hired last week**, will start work on Monday.

We hired *her* last week.

Sheila, **whom you helped for three hours last week**, is very grateful.

You helped *her* for three hours last week.

Our new manager, **whom I know personally**, comes to us from Allied, Inc.

I know *her* personally.

Whom in Prepositional Phrases

Always use **whom** in a prepositional phrase.

She is the person **from whom** I heard the news.

I heard the news from *her*.

When the sentence is in the form of a question, answering the question will usually tell you the correct form. As you word your answer, notice the form of pronoun you select when answering the question. When you would use *she, he, I,* or *they,* to answer the question, use **who**. When you would use *her, him, me,* or *them,* to answer the question, use **whom**.

To whom did you give the results?

I gave the results to *her*.

Remember the preceding rule. Since the pronoun **her** substituted here makes sense grammatically, use *whom*.

With whom are you acquainted at this firm?

I am acquainted with *him*.

To whom did you send the check?

I sent the check to *her*.

Who After a Linking Verb

After a linking verb, you will always find either an adjective that describes the subject or a noun or pronoun that renames the subject.

He did not know **who** the applicant was.

This *who* appears in an adjective clause—*who the applicant was*. The clause already has a subject—*applicant*, but *whom* is not the correct choice—why? Because in re-wording the clause we find that *who* renames *the applicant* after the linking verb *was.—The applicant was **she/he***. The pronoun here *renames* the subject of the adjective clause, so *who* is the correct choice.

Practice and In-Class Exercises

Note: Answers to all practice exercises can be found at the back of the book.

Exercise 19 (Practice)
Who/Whom

Select the correct pronoun form for each sentence.

1. (Who/Whom) did the company send to the meeting?

2. (Who/Whom) will finish the report if Sally leaves early?

3. (Who/Whom) has Miss Dixon appointed as our representative?

4. (Who/Whom) among the staff has the time to manage this project?

5. In the past, (who/whom) did you rate highly?

6. The manager (who/whom) is responsible for the most sales in January will get a bonus.

7. The woman (who/whom) came in late has the data we need.

8. All of the employees (who/whom) we hired last year have adjusted very well to their jobs.

9. Anyone to (who/whom) this announcement applies should see me.

10. The person with (who/whom) I just spoke would like to apply for work here.

Exercise 19 (In Class)

Who/Whom

Select the correct pronoun form for each sentence.

1. We were surprised to hear about Mr. Roberts, in (who/whom) Ms. Jamison trusted completely.

2. (Who/Whom) seems like the best candidate for the position?

3. (Who/Whom) did you go to lunch with today?

4. Mr. Doyle, (who/whom) spoke with you yesterday, would like us to look over the brochure he left for us in the lobby.

5. Mr. Doyle, with (who/whom) you spoke yesterday, would like us to look over the brochure he left for us in the lobby.

6. Many systems analysts (who/whom) we have consulted are unfamiliar with our problem.

7. Mr. Decker, on (who/whom) the decision rests, just took a week off.

8. (Who/Whom) did the vice-president appoint to head the sales department?

9. Mrs. Johnson, (who/whom) you considered for employment, called today to see if the position had been filled.

10. Of the four employees, (who/whom) could best handle the assignment?

MYSELF, HERSELF, HIMSELF

The use of *myself, herself,* and *himself* is very specialized in English. The rule is, unless you have already used *I* in the sentence, you cannot use *myself.* Thus, *Give the report to Bob or myself* is wrong—The word *I* does not appear before the word *myself.*

    wrong   Give the report to Bob or myself.
    right   Give the report to Bob or me.

We somehow become confused about pronoun usage when someone else is mentioned before *I* or *me* in the sentence. The rule, however, does not change simply because a noun or another pronoun precedes *I* or *me.*

We would never say "Give the report to myself," so don't change the form simply because *Bob or* appears in front of *myself.*

    wrong   Gloria, Dave, and myself will work on the project.
    right   Gloria, Dave, and I will work on the project.

Myself can be used appropriately either in a (1) reflexive function or in an (2) intensive function.

Used as an intensive, *myself* merely makes stronger the *I* in the sentence—but the word *myself* could be omitted entirely without changing the meaning of the sentence:

    right   I myself would like to go.
    right   I myself wrote the report.

Myself could also be omitted....

    right   I would like to go.
    right   I wrote the report.

Myself can also be used in a *reflexive* function:

    right   I hurt myself on the sharp edge.

As a reflexive, *myself* cannot be omitted from the sentence, because in this case *myself* tells whom *I* hurt. If *I* hurt someone else, the sentence would read: "I hurt him on the sharp edge." If someone other than *I* did the damage, the sentence would read "She hurt **herself** on the sharp edge."

UNCLEAR PRONOUN REFERENCE

A pronoun such as **this** should not normally be used without the noun to which it refers. When **this** appears alone, the reader is left confused.

unclear   We spent many hours discussing all of the possibilities with Mr. Garvin. **This** appealed to him. This what? To clear up the confusion, add the appropriate word or words immediately after **This**.

clear   We spent many hours discussing all of the possibilities with Mr. Garvin. **This thorough analysis** appealed to him.

unclear   Paul and I spent several hours researching the data and analyzing it. **This** took a long time. This what?

clear   Paul and I spent several hours researching the data and analyzing it. **This process** took a long time.

Practice and In-Class Exercises

Note: Answers to all practice exercises can be found at the back of the book.

Exercise 20 (Practice)
Unclear Pronoun References

Rewrite the following unclear sentences by adding the appropriate noun after *this* or *these*. In some cases, you may need to rewrite the sentence.

1. A large expenditure will be necessary to construct the new warehouse, but this will enable us to reach several new markets.

   _____

   _____

   _____

2. Some of the pages had footnotes, but these were deleted from the final report.

   _____

   _____

   _____

3. Our relocation to the Southwest will require careful planning, but this will be necessary if we are to remain competitive.

   _____

   _____

   _____

   _____

Exercise 20 (In Class)
Unclear Pronoun References

Rewrite the following unclear sentences by adding the appropriate noun after *this* or *these*. In some cases, you may need to rewrite the sentence.

1. Our store credit accounts are in direct competition with bank cards, since our store balance may be carried over with only a minimum monthly payment. This has angered many banks.

_____

_____

_____

2. The seminars include free personalized visual screenings to determine if the patient is a suitable candidate for contact lenses. This is followed up by a video presentation to the patient.

_____

_____

_____

3. I plan to fly in to Houston on Thursday instead of Friday. My manager said this will be O.K. with her.

_____

_____

_____

4. The machine was designed for a moderate volume of use. We are producing a heavy volume. This accounts in part for the excessive downtime due to maintenance problems.

_____

_____

_____

SENTENCE TYPES—
SIMPLE, COMPOUND, AND COMPLEX

You should be familiar with three sentence types for business writing—simple, compound, and complex. Types are determined by the number of stand-alone thoughts (independent clauses) and the number of dependent (or subordinate) clauses. *Remember* that to be called a **clause**, the word group **must** have, at minimum, *one subject and one verb;* otherwise, the word group is called a *phrase*.

Simple Sentences

A **simple** sentence contains **one independent clause** (one subject and one verb (SV), two subjects and one verb (SSV), or one subject and two verbs (SVV) and **no subordinate clauses.**

sc—subordinate conjunction

s/v—subject and verb of subordinate clause

S/V—subject and verb of independent clause

HV—helping verb

    prep phrase   *S*   *V*
On examining the goods, we found them to be defective.

There is only one independent clause here. The first part, *on examining the goods* is a prepositional phrase.

    prep phrase   *S* *V*
After finishing the report, I felt a sense of relief.

    prep phrase   *prep phrase* *S* *HV* *V*
Upon arriving in Portland, he was met at the airport by his friends.

    participial phrase   *S*   *V*
Upset by the noise, he left his desk to find the problem.

            S   *V*
His one ambition was to become manager by the age of 32.

     S   *V*   *gerund*   *gerund*
Friendship means forgetting the bad and remembering the good.

Compound Sentences

A **compound** sentence contains **two independent clauses** (SV/SV) and **no subordinate clauses.** The two independent clauses can be separated by a comma and coordinating conjunction (and, but, or, nor, so), or they can be separated with only a semicolon.

 S   V   S   V
The man is in the office now; he wants to speak to you.

 S   HV   V   S HV   V
A report was presented to the stockholders by the auditor, and it was well received.

              S   V   S V
The vice-president's office is in the corner; it is on the second floor.

            S   V   S
Fast-food restaurants offer their customers many advantages, but the quality of
            V
ingredients isn't one of them.

       S   HV   V   S   V
The meeting was adjourned early, so we went back to work.

Complex Sentences

A **complex** sentence contains **one independent clause** (SV, SSV, SVV) and **one or more subordinate clauses.** A subordinate clause can be one of three types: (1) an adverb clause (beginning with a subordinate conjunction), (2) an adjective clause (beginning with *who, which,* or *that*), or (3) a noun clause (normally beginning with *that* or *what*).

  sc   S   V   S   HV   V
After we voted on several issues, the meeting was adjourned.
  [*sub clause, adverb type*   ] [*independent clause*   ]

 S V   sc   s   lv   lv
She is very much interested in the position although she does not have the right
 [*independent clause*   ] [*sub clause, adverb type*   ]
qualifications.

                    sc   s   lv   S   V
Even though five members were present, we voted to reschedule the meeting.
[sub clause, adverb type   ] [independent clause   ]

                    S   s   v   HV   V
The employees who want to take their vacation in July should submit their request now.
[independent] [sub clause, adjective type   ] [clause   ]

Notice in this example how the adjective clause comes *between* the subject and
verb of the independent clause. Adjective clauses are placed this way quite often. Just remember that the verb of the independent clause is **not** *want*.
Although *employees want* sounds logical, what do you do with the verb that follows—*should submit*? The answer is that *want* is the verb of the adjective
clause only, not of the independent clause.

     S   V SC s   hv   v
He said that you would go to the presentation on January 6.
[ind cl] [subordinate clause, noun type   ]

     S   V   sc   s   hv   v
We gave a gift to Dolores since she is leaving the company at the end of this month.
[independent clause   ] [subordinate clause, adverb type   ]

     S   V   V   sc   s   v
We will have to cancel your order unless we hear from you by Friday, June 13.
[independent clause   ] [subordinate clause, adverb type   ]

          S   V   sc   s   v
Mr. Nelson told us that integrity in an employee is extremely important.
[independent clause] [subordinate clause, noun type   ]

               S   s   v   v   HV HV V
Our February report, which is being typed by John, will be sent to you tomorrow.
[independent   [sub clause, adjective type]   clause   ]

S   V   sc   s   v
I tried for several hours to analyze the results that Rich gave me.
[independent clause   ] [subordinate clause, adjective type]

Practice and In-Class Exercises

Note: Answers to all practice exercises can be found at the back of the book.

Exercise 21 (Practice)
Types of Sentences

Identify the following sentences as either simple, compound, or complex.

1. We are writing to acknowledge receipt of the May 3 shipment.

2. I wish you and the rest of the committee the greatest success in achieving the goals set this year.

3. I wanted to finish the project ahead of schedule, so we stayed until midnight to finish it.

4. He prepared appropriate graphics and practiced his presentation thoroughly.

5. To stay within our budget, we will have to limit purchases for office supplies this month.

6. When you apply for the position, include a cover letter with your resume.

7. He terminated the project when first quarter results began to look unfavorable.

8. If Harry feels strongly about his decision, ask him to write me a memo stating his position.

9. Our records indicate that you are behind in your payments.

10. If the customer calls within the next few days, get his new telephone number.

11. Marty told the engineers last week that the specifications had been changed.

12. I talked with Heather in Accounting about implementing this idea, and she was very supportive.

Exercise 21 (In Class)
Types of Sentences

Identify the following sentences as either simple, compound, or complex.

1. We are pleased to offer you a position on our staff of skilled and well-educated employees.

2. I resigned yesterday and began my job search today.

3. The recent decision was based on changes in our accounting procedures.

4. I became manager before Arnie joined the company.

5. Pauline brought up her main objection to the plan after the meeting ended.

6. Ms. Arnold explained the project; most of those in attendance disagreed with the idea.

7. He added three more sections to the report because his supervisor told him to do it.

8. Although we have given him several orders recently, he still seems unsatisfied.

9. Marsha cannot finish the assignment this week because she is flying to Philadelphia on Friday.

10. Riding the bus to work saves gas and clears the freeways of traffic.

11. All of our new employees must attend an orientation session this Friday in Conference Room A.

12. Your representative has been briefed on these procedures, and she will be able to answer your questions.

13. For the second quarter, the Eastern Division reported revenues of $835,500.

14. The parts that were shipped from New York should arrive on Tuesday.

SENTENCE FRAGMENTS

When a sentence is missing either a subject or verb or both, it is said to be a *fragment*, meaning a fragment of a sentence. Fragments are confusing because they lack a main point.

wrong   By accepting the idea of efficiency.

           Prepositional phrase only—missing both subject and verb

right   By accepting the idea of efficiency, we began to make several major changes.

           Added a subject and verb

wrong   My manager, Mr. John Sparks, who came to the company only last year.

           Subject, appositive (see glossary for the definition of appositives), adjective-type subordinate clause...but no verb—the verb of the subordinate clause (*came*) cannot also be the verb of the independent clause.

right   My manager, Mr. John Sparks, who came to the company only last year, died yesterday.

           Added an independent-clause verb, *died*

wrong   Cynthia, looking very worried and perplexed.

           Subject, participial phrase describing her, but no verb.

right   Cynthia, looking very worried and perplexed, sat in silence for another 20 minutes.

           Added verb

wrong   Failing to give his employer proper notice.

           A participial phrase, performing an adjective function; the sentence is missing both subject and verb

right   Failing to give his employer proper notice, John left the company yesterday.

           Added a subject and verb

wrong   As soon as we receive the results and double-check the figures.

Subordinate clause standing alone as an independent clause—it has one subject and two verbs, but because the clause begins with a subordinate conjunction, *as soon as,* the clause can **never** be an independent clause, no matter what words you put after the subordinate conjunction.

right   As soon as we receive the results and double-check the figures, we will give you a call.

Added an independent clause.

wrong   When she had no one to turn to.

Subordinate clause only—it cannot stand alone as an independent clause.

right   When she had no one to turn to, she turned to me.

Added independent clause—stand-alone subject and verb.

Dangling Modifiers

Dangling modifiers are another type of sentence construction error, sometimes causing reader confusion, sometimes reader laughter, and sometimes only slight misunderstanding.

A dangling modifier can occur when you begin a sentence with an infinitive phrase, a prepositional phrase, or a participial phrase. In each of these constructions, you have not yet identified the subject of the sentence—remember, phrases have no subject. Therefore, *the first word following* the introductory phrase **must** be the subject implied in the phrase.

Note: This information does *not* apply to introductory subordinate clauses. Since clauses, by definition, contain a subject and verb, they cannot potentially *dangle*.

Dangling

> To get the most out of our time here today, the session will include a discussion of several problems you are facing.

The sentence begins with an infinitive phrase—no subject is mentioned. What follows the comma must be *who* is to get the most out of our time here today.

The construction is illogical as it stands. In English, we assume that the word following the comma is who/what you were talking about in the introductory phrase. In this case, it appears that *the session* will get the most out of the time...., and that is an illogical idea.

To straighten out the logic, grammatically, either turn the introductory infinitive phrase into a subordinate clause (adding an appropriate subject and verb), or put the correct subject after the comma:

Correction #1—turn the introductory phrase into an introductory subordinate clause:

> **So that we can get the most out of our time together here today**, the session will include a discussion of several problems you are facing.

Correction #2—keep the introductory phrase as is, but replace the first word after the phrase with the correct subject:

To get the most out of our time together here today, **we** will include in this session a discussion of several problems you are facing.

Dangling

After looking at the new cars for a while, the salesman walked toward me.

The introductory prepositional phrase has no subject. The word following the phrase must be who was looking at the cars—it isn't the salesman but someone else. To correct the incorrect logic, change the sentence structure in one of two ways:

Correction #1—turn the introductory phrase into an introductory subordinate clause:

After I had looked at the new cars for a while, the salesman walked toward me.

Correction #2—keep the introductory phrase as is, but replace the first word after the phrase with a logical subject:

After looking at the new cars for a while, **I saw the salesman walk toward me.**

Dangling

While working late in the office, Jeremy's car was burglarized in the parking lot.

The sentence construction implies that Jeremy's car was working late in the office. This idea is illogical. To correct the faulty logic, change the sentence construction in one of two ways:

Correction #1—turn the introductory phrase into an introductory subordinate clause:

While Jeremy was working late in the office, his car was burglarized in the parking lot.

also changed the independent clause slightly to fit better

Correction #2—keep the introductory phrase as is, but replace the first word after the phrase with the correct subject:

While working late in the office, **Jeremy** had his car burglarized in the parking lot.

This re-write isn't as effective as Correction #1.

Dangling

Completely renovated, I hardly recognized the old building.

The construction implies that *I* was completely renovated. Obviously, this meaning is incorrect. To correct the problem, restructure the sentence in either of two ways:

Correction #1—turn the introductory phrase into an introductory subordinate clause (i.e., add a subject and verb):

Since the old building had been completely renovated, I hardly recognized it.

or

Correction #2—keep the introductory phrase as is, but replace the first word after the phrase with the correct subject the words describe:

Completed renovated, the old building was difficult to recognize.

The meaning is changed somewhat with the rewrite, but the sentence is at least correct.

Misplaced Modifiers

A misplaced modifier is a word, phrase, or clause that modifies or describes another word in the sentence but is located in the wrong place. Words are thought to modify whatever word or words they are placed closest to in the sentence. When a group of words is not placed next to the word it describes, confusion or misunderstanding is often created:

wrong   We purchased a desk in Los Angeles last year at a discount store **that cost less than $500**.

That cost less than $500 is an adjective clause that modifies *desk*. It was the desk that cost less than $500, not a discount store. Because the adjective clause was placed closest to *discount store,* the reader may assume it was the discount store that cost less than $500. This, of course, is not what was meant. To correct the misunderstanding, move the adjective clause so that it immediately follows what it describes—a desk.

right   We purchased a desk **that cost less than $500** at a discount store in Los Angeles.

The sentence was reworded in other places, too, for improved understanding.

wrong   We anticipate **next year** that the economy will improve.

What do the words *next year* go with? Do we anticipate next year that...? or do we anticipate that the economy will improve *next year*? Obviously, it's the latter.

right   We anticipate that the economy will improve **next year**.

wrong   Darla found some confidential memos written by her manager **in the conference room.**

It is unlikely that the manager sat in the conference room to write the confidential memos. If that is true, it is better to say

Darla found some confidential memos which her manager wrote in the conference room.

If her manager did *not* write the memos in the conference room, change the wording to avoid misunderstanding:

right Darla found **in the conference** room some confidential memos written by her manager.

or

In the conference room, Darla found some confidential memos written by her manager.

wrong We ordered seven new file cabinets from the factory in Detroit **made of walnut**.

It wasn't Detroit that was made of walnut, but the file cabinets. Move the modifying phrase next to the word it describes:

right We ordered seven new file cabinets **made of walnut** from the factory in Detroit.

or

We ordered seven new **walnut** file cabinets from the factory in Detroit.

This version is a little more concise than the previous one.

Where Do These Words Belong?

Where words are placed in the sentence can make a big difference in the meaning:

I told Brian **this morning** to add three more graphics to our presentation.

I asked for this in the morning, or, possibly, he should do it this morning. It is difficult to know for sure, because the two words appear between the request *I told* and what I told him to do. This is called a *squinting* modifier because the words could go with *I told Brian* or *to add three more graphics*. This construction should be avoided because of the misunderstanding it can create.

I told Brian to add three more graphics **this morning** to our presentation.

This structure is more clear. It doesn't say when I told him this, but it tells when I want him to do it—this morning he should add the three graphics.

This morning I told Brian to add three more graphics to our presentation.

This is now clear as to when I told him but not as to when he should complete the task. I told him this morning to add more graphics, but how much time does he have to do it? It isn't stated.

I told Brian to add three more graphics to our presentation **this morning**.

This placement implies that the presentation is to occur this morning. Obviously, he would also have to add the three graphics sometime the same morning before the presentation.

Be Careful Where You Place the Word Only

If you plan to use the word *only* in a sentence, be sure you put it in the correct place. The word must be placed next to the word or words it describes or limits. You could, theoretically, put the word *only* in 4 different places in the following sentence:

My supervisor told me to finish the job before noon.

Where the *only* is placed can significantly change the meaning of the thought:

Only my supervisor told me to finish the job before noon.
No one but my supervisor told me this.

My supervisor told **only** me to finish the job before noon.
She didn't tell anyone else.

My supervisor told me to finish the **only** job before noon.
There was just one job to complete—no more.

My supervisor told me to finish the job **only** before noon.
I can finish the job any time up to noon—even one minute before. It is better to change *only* to *any time*.

Practice and In-Class Exercises

Note: Answers to all practice exercises can be found at the back of the book.

Exercise 22 (Practice)

Dangling Modifiers, Misplaced Modifiers, and Sentence Fragments

In the sentences that follow, identify and correct any dangling modifiers, misplaced modifiers, or sentence fragments. Some sentences may be correct as written. Remember, a dangling modifier begins with an introductory phrase (prepositional, participial, or infinitive) and is followed by the *wrong* subject.

A misplaced modifier is simply in the wrong place in the sentence. Circle the misplaced words and draw an arrow to where they should be put.

1. By following these procedures, the process will take very little time.

2. In concluding the report, recommendations were added by Marianne Jones.

3. Rick Rodgers thought until December 1 we were still a subsidiary of Davidson Corporation.

4. Although Bill had a great deal of difficulty making the new software package work.

5. After I had been rejected by three companies, my employment counselor suggested I rewrite my resume.

6. Jack threatened to leave the company often.

7. Alert for errors, the mistake was caught by my secretary.

8. To provide maximum coverage, you must have a comprehensive policy.

9. Since the report is due in my manager's office two weeks from today.

10. Last month the Capitol was closed for renovations to all visitors.

11. Although the order was placed on August 3, it has not yet been received.

12. Reaching for the butter, his water glass fell over.

13. The contracts, signed by all parties.

Exercise 22 (In Class)
Dangling Modifiers, Misplaced Modifiers, and Sentence Fragments

In the sentences that follow, identify and correct any dangling modifiers, misplaced modifiers, or sentence fragments. Some sentences may be correct as written. Remember, a dangling modifier begins with an introductory phrase (prepositional, participial, or infinitive) and is followed by the *wrong* subject.

A misplaced modifier is simply in the wrong place in the sentence. Circle the misplaced words and draw an arrow to where they should be put.

1. Moving to Florida, his lung problems quickly improved.

2. To save money, the thermostat must be turned down to 70 degrees.

3. To receive full retirement benefits, the pension plan must be participated in for 20 years.

4. Several of the branch managers, planning to attend this year's conference.

5. Ms. Kawakita mailed the firm a check that had reroofed the building.

6. Johnston Products is seeking applicants with excellent communication skills.

7. Ms. Marks, who would not have been able to complete the assignment without Mr. Thorsen's help.

8. After waiting six weeks for the test results, concern grew that the results would not be favorable.

9. Myra sent a proposal to the manager for improving office productivity.

10. To use time properly, prepare an agenda before the meeting.

11. Even though Mr. Benson wrote the entire report himself.

12. Steve Sawyer, the employee that Mr. Williams selected as the employee of the month.

13. The memo was sent to all salespeople about recent product line changes last week.

14. Employees want recognition for a job well done from management.

COMMA RULES

1. ***Use a comma before a coordinating conjunction*** (and, but, or, nor, so) ***that joins two independent clauses (SV/SV).***

S/V—subject and verb of independent clause

HV—helping verb—part of verb phrase

cc—coordinating conjunction

    S   V   cc   S   V
He arrived yesterday, **and** the conference began today.

          S   V   cc S V
My manager stayed late, **so** I know that he had the time to finish my performance appraisal.

S HV   V   cc HV S V
I didn't want to respond to the question, **nor** did I want to ask one.

S   V   cc S HV   V
I covered that point in my report, **but** I didn't cover it thoroughly enough.

Note: *Do not separate words or phrases joined by* and *or* or:

    wrong   He went to the office, and opened his mail.

    right   He went to the office and opened his mail. (no comma)

    right   He went to the office, and he opened his mail.

            Addition of *he* after *and* creates a compound sentence. Rule 1 now applies, requiring the comma before *and*.

Note: *Do not place a required comma after the conjunction:*

    wrong   She was tired but, she refused to stop working.

    right   She was tired, but she refused to stop working.

Note: Do not interrupt the normal flow of thought by a comma:

wrong   The fact that the contract was not submitted on time, was the reason my manager was upset.

right   The fact that the contract was not submitted on time was the reason my manager was upset.

wrong   The newly hired consultant insisted, that he knew what he was doing. (remove comma—uncalled for—no rule for this)

right   The newly hired consultant insisted that he knew what he was doing. (no comma)

2. ***Use a comma to separate the elements in a series.*** *(Be sure to include the comma before the and.)*

nouns in a series

I brought a pencil, pen, calculator, and paper to the meeting.

adjectives in a series

Her shirt was red, white, and blue.

verb phrases in a series

He came in late, spent one hour having coffee, talked for two hours on the phone, and took three hours for lunch.

infinitives in a series

She wanted to read, to study, and to perform well on the exam.

prepositional phrases in a series

We advertise in newspapers, on radio, and over television.

adverbs in a series

He slowly, painstakingly, and nervously walked to the front of the room.

3. ***Use a comma to set off an introductory single word.***

Historically, profit margins have been low.

Fortunately, I had the answer.

Undoubtedly, you know my manager.

Yes, we will attend.

No, we cannot accept your offer.

True, we have no reason to object to the plan.

Luckily, our restaurant chains are in a strong position.

4. *Use a comma to set off an introductory phrase—infinitive, prepositional, or participial.*

Examples of introductory phrases

Introductory infinitive phrase (to + verb root):

To get the most from our product, you need to follow all instructions carefully.

To assure herself of a passing grade, Cheryl spent most of the weekend studying.

To secure the attention of his audience, the speaker shouted in a commanding voice.

To accommodate my fellow workers, I took my vacation in October.

Introductory prepositional phrase (one or more before the independent clause):

Note: The prepositional phrase does *not* contain a verb. If the structure contains a verb, it is a clause.

```
[      1      ][    2    ]
```
Before returning to New York, my manager called me three times from the airport.

After mastering BASIC, Connie went on to learn PASCAL and FORTRAN.

Since yesterday, I have had to deal with three emergencies in the department.

Against my better judgment, I agreed to try John's idea.

Underneath it all, I like my new manager.

```
[     1     ][   2   ]
```
Without a copy of the report, I was lost.

```
[     1     ][   2   ]
```
Beneath the stack of papers, I found the figures I was looking for.

In my opinion, municipal bonds are an excellent investment.

[*1*   ][*2*   ]
With the right combination of luck and wisdom, we should succeed.

During the strike, there will be shortages of some items.

[*1*   ][*2*]
Upon arriving in Dallas, he was met at the airport by his friends.

Introductory participial phrase (past, present, or perfect participle used as an adjective, *not* as a verb):

perf part
Having worked in Farmingdale's for several years, I know the types of sales promotions they normally run.

pres part
Hoping to win favor with his manager, he volunteered to give the presentation.

pres part
Completing her report, Marsha went home early.

pres part
Speaking off the record, the vice-president told us about the plan.

pres part
Running to catch the bus, Marvin tripped.

pres part
Seeing his chance for success, Jacob immediately accepted the assignment.

pres part
Working quickly, she carefully planned her opening remarks.

Occasionally, a participle will be used singly as an adjective:

past part
Agitated, she stomped from the room.

past part
Relieved, she began to talk of more pleasant things.

pres part
Smiling, my manager gave us the good news.

Be sure to set off with commas a participial phrase wherever it occurs in the sentence:

pres part

Mr. Benson, *noting my lack of confidence*, gave me some pointers to reduce my nervousness.

pres part

David, *reporting the changes to me daily,* was surprised with my decision.

past part

Deborah, *surprised by the interruption*, didn't know what to say.

past p

Reprographics, *also known as reproduction or duplication,* and fax represent other forms of word processing output.

This participial phrase begins with an *adverb*.

pres part

Stan, *discovering an error in his computations*, immediately called his manager.

pres part

He opened a savings account, *looking to the future.*

5. *Use a comma to set off an introductory subordinate clause.*

Examples of Introductory Subordinate Clauses :

These clauses have a subject and verb and are all *dependent* or *subordinate*—they cannot stand alone as a complete thought. *All subordinate clauses begin with a subordinate conjunction* such as

after	because	while
as	so that	whenever
as soon	as if	until
as long as	unless	whether
before	although	when
since	that	while

sc—subordinate conjunction

s/v—subject and verb of subordinate clause

S/V—subject and verb of independent clause

HV—helping verb

   sc s   v   S V

After I finished the report, I made three phone calls.

   ——sc—— s v   S HV V

As soon as we get the figures from Purchasing, we can write this section of the report.

sc s hv   v   S HV HV V

If you are willing to make the initial investment, you will be amply repaid.

   sc s   v   S HV V

Unless sales increase dramatically in the fourth quarter, we will suffer our first loss since 1970.

  sc   s v   S HV V

Since we started the project last March, much has happened.

sc s   v   S HV V

If you insist, I will chair the committee.

   sc   s v   S V

Whenever Mr. Johnson arrives late, the meeting runs overtime.

  sc   s hv   v   S—you V

So that we can process your order quickly,   complete the enclosed card.

   sc s   v   S   V (that)

After we finished lunch, Mr. Henderson suggested we adjourn to his office to continue the discussion.

sc s v   S HV V

If we pay full tuition now, we can get a discount rate.

   sc   s   v   S   V

While hardware refers to the computer itself, software refers to a system or program to achieve efficient use of a computer.

Some subordinate clauses, rather than appearing at the beginning of the sentence, may intervene in the middle of the sentence. If they are used this way, set them off with commas:

Several of us, **because we heard the report,** expressed concern about the company's future.

I have decided, **even if I get a raise,** to look for another job.

6. *Use a comma to set off a parenthetical or transitional expression or word.*

A parenthetical expression is a word or phrase which is abruptly inserted in a sentence and interrupts the natural flow of the sentence. Sometimes these expressions are referred to as *interrupters*. Such expressions could be removed without changing the meaning of the sentence. To show that the word or expression is nonessential, set the expression or word off with commas. Some examples of parenthetical expressions or *interrupters* are

as a consequence	I believe	as a result
if necessary	as a rule	in addition
of course	in brief	on the contrary
as you know	in fact	on the other hand
by the way	for example	together with_____
at any rate	besides	then
it has been said	in my opinion	finally
accordingly	consequently	in other words
personally	respectively	that is
naturally	obviously	

We are certain, **then**, that you will comply with our request.

The test results will, **I believe**, confirm our position.

Familiarity, **it has been said**, breeds contempt.

Mr. Morgan, **by the way**, used to work in our Pittsburgh office.

We can, **in fact**, meet the shipment date.

Bill has not put much time into the project; Steve, **on the other hand**, has worked many weekends.

It is, **in our opinion**, impossible to predict the outcome at this moment.

No one, **naturally**, can be blamed for such an innocent mistake.

The major obstacle to this alternative, **obviously**, is the required allocation of $15 million in investment capital.

I believe, **for example**, that a brusque answer does much harm and little good.

We feel, **therefore**, that an immediate decision is essential.

Feel free, **of course**, to take as much time as you need.

It is, **however**, unnecessary for you to reply at once.

We can't, **as a rule**, send packages by Federal Express.

He was told, **it seems**, that no more money would be available.

Margaret, **by the way**, has several excellent ideas for improving customer service.

The new engine, **together with a small box of tools**, will be shipped to you on Wednesday.

Our firm has, **I believe**, the industry's most efficient system.

The costs of complete retooling, **however**, are extremely high.

7. *Use a comma to set off a noun or nouns in direct address.*

Direct address means that you speak directly to someone in your sentence, as if you were having a face-to-face conversation, calling that person by name.

Examples of nouns in direct address:

Ladies and gentlemen, prepare yourselves for the worst.

I don't know the answer, **Lisa**.

Ms. Davidson, please take a number and be seated.

I think, **Michael**, that we can solve this problem in one of several ways.

In preparing this report, **Ms. Huston**, the study team analyzed two years' worth of data.

Mark and Lonnie, your schedules have been changed.

8. *Use a comma to set off a nonessential appositive.*

An appositive is a word or small group of words immediately after a noun that further describes the noun but does not include a verb. An appositive is considered unnecessary to the sentence (nonessential) when the noun it describes is already specifically defined.

Examples of nonessential appositives:

Our city's busiest street, **Jackson Avenue**, will be resurfaced in March.

Charles P. Langdon, **our leading candidate for mayor**, is a brilliant business executive.

My only son, **Wayne**, would like to practice corporation law.

My son Wayne would like to practice corporation law.

In this case, commas are omitted around Wayne because his name is needed to know *which* son is being spoken of. This sentence is an example of an essential appositive.

Our assistant cashier, **Ruth Burke**, would like to apply for the position.

Phyllis Cosgrove, **Mr. Franco's assistant**, has taken a leave of absence.

Mr. Laughlin, **the newest vice-president**, was hired by our Denver office.

In his remarks, the president referred to Debra Miller, **our office manager**.

Mr. Collins and Ms. Chen, **both Princeton graduates**, disagreed as to the strategy we should employ.

Our top sales manager, **Don Collier**, left for Chicago yesterday.

9. *Use a comma to set off a nonessential adjective clause.*

An adjective clause describes a noun in the sentence. If the noun is not specific, the adjective clause is needed to further specify the noun. If the noun is already very specific, the adjective clause adds only supplementary information and so is nonessential. **If the noun is already very specific, set off the adjective clause with commas.**

The pair of commas around a nonessential clause functions much like a pair of parentheses—you want to let the reader know that what is inside the commas is supplementary information only.

To determine if the clause is nonessential (or unnecessary), look at the word the clause modifies—usually the last word before the clause begins. If the word it modifies is specific enough, you can omit the clause without changing the meaning of the sentence.

If the word is vague or non-specific, you will change the meaning of the sentence if you indicate with commas that the clause can be removed. If the word the clause refers to is not specific, you need the clause for further clarification, so you would *not* use commas around the clause.

Here are some examples of adjective clauses that are *not necessary* to understanding the sentence—that is, the noun the clause refers to is already specific enough:

George Yamamoto, **who sells real estate in our office,** can probably answer your question.

George Yamamoto is specific enough as a subject that you don't need *who sells real estate* to further define him.

> *(that)*
> Analysts said many traders were concerned that the stock market, **which hit record highs recently**, was due for a more pronounced pullback.

The noun *stock market* is specific enough that you don't need the adjective clause **which hit record highs recently**. Since the clause is not needed to make the *stock market* clear, the clause is considered nonessential and is surrounded by commas.

> Intel, **which was once owned by IBM**, is a major manufacturer of semiconductors, microprocessors, and microcomputers.

The clause **which was once owned by IBM** refers to the noun *Intel*. *Intel* is specific enough, so we don't need the clause for further clarification; therefore, set off the clause, or surround it, with commas to show that the clause could be omitted from the sentence with no change in meaning.

> A copy of this year's balance sheet, **which had already been audited**, was attached to the agenda.

This year's balance sheet is specific enough that you don't need the *which* clause for further identification; therefore, the *which* clause serves only as supplementary information—set it off with commas.

> Marci, **who is an expert in this field**, will lead the discussion.

The clause **who is an expert in this field** is not necessary to further define *Marci*. There is only one Marci; therefore, the relative clause **who is an expert in this field** is nonessential and could be removed from the sentence without changing the meaning. Set off the clause with commas to show that the clause is merely additional detail.

The following are examples of essential adjective clauses—these are needed in the sentence because the noun they refer to is *not* specific enough. The additional information supplied by the clause is needed to fully understand the noun being spoken about.

> The person **who is considerate of others** will never lack friends.

Person is too vague —it needs the clause **who is considerate of others** to further specify *person*. When the clause *is* needed for further clarification of the word it modifies, *do not* set off the clause with commas. You *cannot* take out the clause without changing the meaning of the sentence.

> Food **that is spoiled** is bad for you.

If you remove **that is spoiled** and say *Food is bad for you,* you have changed the meaning entirely. This sentence, then, needs the adjective clause to make clear *which* kind of food is bad for you, so do not put commas around the adjective clause.

> You should use the printer **that is in my office.**

Essential, necessary clause—to remove the clause would change the meaning of the sentence. You should not use any printer, only the one in my office, so *no* comma after *printer*.

> People **who are continually late to work** usually have difficulties
> getting along with their manager.

People as a subject here is imprecise. We need the adjective clause to further define which kind of people have difficulties with their manager. If you surround the clause with commas, you are suggesting that the clause *could* be removed without changing the meaning of the sentence. If you did remove the clause, it would read

> People usually have difficulties getting along with their manager.

This is not at all the same thing—not all people have the difficulty, only those who are continually late to work; thus, you must keep the clause for clarification, so do not put commas around the adjective clause.

10. *Use a comma to set off a linking adverb after a semicolon.*

A linking adverb links or joins two independent clauses.

Examples of linking adverbs

also	however	nevertheless
furthermore	therefore	consequently
in addition	thus	

The book is excellent; **however**, its price is too high.

The shipment arrived yesterday; **however**, it is incomplete.

The materials arrived late; **therefore**, the secretary didn't type the report today.

He spoke with great enthusiasm; **consequently**, he convinced many people of several bad ideas.

On weekdays we close at 7 p.m.; **however**, on weekends we stay open until 11 p.m.

Everyone arrived for the meeting on time; **nevertheless**, it still ran overtime.

The growth in profits last year was largely due to the opening of ten new sales territories; **however**, only two new territories were opened this year.

11. *Use a comma between two equal-ranking adjectives in front of one noun.*

To determine whether the adjectives are *equal,* connect them with *and*. If the two adjectives sound just as appropriate when connected with *and,* they are considered equal, so a comma between them (if you omit the *and*) is the rule.

She is an intelligent, determined woman.

She is an intelligent and determined woman.
Still sounds correct.

She supervises seven senior accountants.
Seven and *senior* could both be considered adjectives here, but are they *equal?*

Try the *and* test:

She supervises seven and senior accountants.
It sounds strange to join the two adjectives with *and,* so *no comma* here—the two words are not considered *equal-ranking adjectives*.

She is engaged in **dangerous, exciting** work.

He is a **thoughtful, introspective** person.

David gave an **insightful, moving** presentation.

12. *Use a comma to separate the parts of dates and addresses.*

The company moved to 1260 Turner Street, Boston, MA, sometime last year.

On May 14, 1968, we celebrated our 40th year in business.

The planning meeting is scheduled for Tuesday, July 10, 1990, in Conference Room D.

We will hold three, consecutive product demonstrations on Wednesday, September 13, at the Hilton Hotel.

Note: Do not use a comma between the month and year if the day of the month is missing:

We began business in May 1967.

Practice and In-Class Exercises

Note: Answers to all practice exercises can be found at the back of the book.

Exercise 23 (Practice)
Comma Usage

For each sentence, state the rule for the comma(s) used.

---

1. two independent clauses joined by a coordinating conjunction
2. items in a series—which type?
3. introductory single word
4. introductory phrase (prepositional, infinitive, participial)
5. introductory subordinate (dependent) clause
6. parenthetical or transitional expression or word
7. noun in direct address
8. nonessential appositive
9. nonessential adjective clause
10. linking adverb
11. two equal-ranking adjectives before a noun
12. date/address

---

1. Sharon ran off the copies, David collated them, and Sherry stapled and distributed them.

2. We will leave immediately after lunch on Thursday, and the seminar begins Friday morning.

3. Our conference rooms need refurbishing, but we don't have money in the budget to do it right now.

4. We tried, but we failed.

5. In spite of your advice, I accepted their offer.

6. What are we doing right, and how can we do it better?

7. During the holiday season, there will be shortages of some items.

8. With your approval of the following specifications, we can begin implementation immediately.

9. Because of your interest in the project, I am making you project leader.

10. You need to learn to write, to compose, and to dictate letters effectively.

11. We have made a good start, but we have a long way to go.

12. Before returning to the office, I have several errands to do.

13. We think, Arlene, that you would be happier working for Ken in Personnel.

14. Arnold, my only brother, applied for work here last June.

15. This firm, which began operations in the valley five years ago, is doing very well financially.

16. You are an excellent supervisor, Chris.

17. The speech turned out to be a boring, tedious one.

18. Ms. Lansing, if you have any questions before or during installation, please call us.

19. She applied for the position, but she did not get it.

20. This morning we received a report from Mr. Talbot, our New York representative.

21. The speaker was Belinda Masters, city councilwoman.

22. Rushing to catch the train, he tripped and sprained his ankle.

23. After hearing about the merger, I began to fear for my job.

24. It is, however, unnecessary for you to work late tonight.

25. It is, in my opinion, impossible to predict the results.

26. Yes, they did report on time.

27. We feel, therefore, that immediate changes are necessary.

28. The firm moved to Sacramento, California, last year.

29. It is, nevertheless, important that your representative phone us immediately.

30. To remain competitive, we need to develop at least two new products this year.

Exercise 23 (In Class)
Comma Usage

For each sentence, state the rule for the comma(s) used.

1. two independent clauses joined by a coordinating conjunction
2. items in a series—which type?
3. introductory single word
4. introductory phrase (prepositional, infinitive, participial)
5. introductory subordinate (dependent) clause
6. parenthetical or transitional expression or word
7. noun in direct address
8. nonessential appositive
9. nonessential adjective clause
10. linking adverb
11. two equal-ranking adjectives before a noun
12. date/address

1. Mail the enclosed card now; however, you will not hear the results for another month.

2. Every lesson in the manual is simple, and every principle is outlined in detail.

3. Tact, wisdom, and diplomacy are all important skills that managers need to possess.

4. Ask questions politely, listen to details carefully, and follow instructions closely.

5. She found an ancient, rusty adding machine in the storage closet.

6. Since we started the project, much has changed.

7. Our sale on computer accessories ends this Saturday, so now is the time to buy.

8. If you are willing to submit a resume, we will consider you for the position.

9. Hoping to find a secure and well-paying job, Cheryl applied to three large corporations.

10. Yes, ladies and gentlemen, this point is important.

11. Jack Anderson, our Harvard graduate, could not solve the problem either.

12. Realizing that it was too late to make a change, George submitted the report unfinished.

13. Sharon, the newest employee, still looks lost.

14. As a rule, Mr. Walters doesn't accept orders without proper authorization.

15. I am convinced, however, that we could have won the contract.

16. Personally, I dislike that man.

17. To accommodate my manager, I offered to work this Sunday.

18. Against all odds, we made a sizable profit this quarter.

19. Mr. Raymond Clayton, who began work here in September, was recently promoted to department manager.

20. Looking beyond the moment, I could see that this problem was really a minor one.

21. So that Glenda could get away early, I offered to finish her paperwork.

22. When employees arrive late, they have to explain to Mr. Jorgensen.

23. If you are willing to put in long hours, you can move up quickly at this company.

24. I believe, Mr. Angelo, that we have an excellent product.

25. Our office opened in San Francisco on July 23, 1990, and has been doing very well ever since.

26. Before we lose sight of our objective, let's think this problem through one more time.

27. The two men discussed their differences for several hours, but they were not able to come to any agreement.

28. That report, in fact, contains some serious errors.

29. Our assistant manager, Ms. Rourke, has been with the company for six months.

30. Karen always gives insightful, interesting presentations.

SEMICOLON USAGE

Use a semicolon in the following situations: (1) to separate two independent clauses in one sentence not joined by a coordinating conjunction (*and, but, or, nor, so*); (2) to separate two independent clauses joined by a linking adverb or parenthetical expression; (3) to separate items in a series when the items themselves have internal commas (to avoid confusion).

1. *To separate two independent clauses in one sentence not joined by a coordinating conjunction.*

   S   V   S   V
   John hurried to finish the report; it was two days late.

   S   V   S   V
   Mary presented an excellent idea; several people agreed with her.

   S   V   S V
   Mark arrived early; I did not.

   To use a comma instead of a semicolon in the preceding examples is *wrong.*

2. *To separate two independent clauses in one sentence connected by a linking adverb or parenthetical expression.*

   S LV LV   S   V
   You will be happy with the results; **in fact**, I guarantee it.

   *   S   HV   V   S   HV   V*
   The deadline has passed; **therefore**, we have cancelled our order.

   S HV   V
   I have listened to your approach for 30 minutes; **however,**

   S   V
   I still disagree with you.

3. *To separate items in a series when the items themselves contain internal commas.*

   We received responses from Portland, Oregon; Los Angeles, California;
   Bangor, Maine; and Anchorage, Alaska.

   The attendees were Marsha Simpson, Marketing; Jane Bolton,
   Purchasing; David Dyer, Sales; and Tom Parkerson, Personnel.

Practice and In-Class Exercises

Note: Answers to all practice exercises can be found at the back of the book.

Exercise 24 (Practice)

Semicolon and Comma Usage

Insert commas and/or semicolons as needed in the following sentences. (Some sentences require no additional punctuation.)

1. Payment is due within 30 days of the billing date you can however save 2% by paying within 10 days.

2. Sue gave an excellent summary to her presentation but it was too long.

3. In light of current legalities however we cannot make specific comments about previous employees.

4. Sandra Holden was not suited to personnel work therefore she was transferred to sales.

5. The meeting began at 8 A.M. she didn't arrive until 8:30.

6. The marketing department has been strong since Nancy took over as manager last May.

7. We like to hold conferences in San Francisco it is an interesting city.

8. David and Marjorie split the assignment and they worked overtime to complete it.

9. Our committee consists of David Anderson Personnel Mary Brown Accounting and Tom Briscott Marketing.

10. Mark looked over the report for errors but could not find any.

11. Because 200 well-qualified candidates applied for the position the selection process was very difficult.

Exercise 24 (In Class)

Semicolon and Comma Usage

Insert commas and/or semicolons as needed in the following sentences. (Some sentences require no additional punctuation.)

1. The odds were insurmountable nevertheless we didn't give up.

2. The doors open at 5 P.M. however you may be admitted at 4:30.

3. Our firm is only five years old but we have established an excellent reputation.

4. Send copies to Joe Standish Rob Langley and Sherry Tilden.

5. The market went up for some stocks other stocks however declined.

6. This is a coincidence I was just speaking to her on the phone.

7. We hired new people on March 31 1989 April 10 1990 and August 16 1990.

8. Your account is over six months past due we cannot therefore extend you further credit.

9. The new printers were ordered two weeks ago they should arrive by the end of the month.

10. Mr. Rankin spoke to Cynthia after the meeting he looked irate.

11. We would like to convince the unions to make some wage and benefit concessions but they're protected by contracts for another six months.

12. We will be introducing two new product lines this year and expect to increase profits 25%.

COLON USAGE

Use a colon in the following situations: (1) after the salutation in a business letter and (2) to begin a list or enumeration when you have preceded the list with a complete thought. (The list or enumeration could be in horizontal or vertical form.)

Example of Rule (1)

Dear Mr. Ruiz:

Dear Gerry:

Dear Ms. Salazar:

Example of Rule (2)

Colon required—(Complete thought before the list)

Please bring the following to the meeting on January 12:

1. last year's budget

2. this year's budget

3. next year's projections

No colon required—(No complete thought before the list)

Please bring to the meeting on January 12

1. last year's budget

2. this year's budget

3. next year's projections

Colon Needed Here—(Complete thought before the list)

If you would like to be considered for this position, you must provide the following: (1) a current resume, (2) a cover letter, (3) a completed application, and (4) three letters of recommendation.

No Colon Here—(No complete thought before the list)

If you would like to be considered for this position, you must provide (1) a current resume, (2) a cover letter, (3) a completed application, and (4) three letters of recommendation.

No Colon Here—(No complete thought before the list)

We did not make a profit this quarter because our competition increased, we lost several sales representatives, and we experienced an economic downturn.

To make the reasons stand out, you could enumerate them:

We did not make a profit this quarter because (1) our competition increased, (2) we lost several sales representatives, and (3) we experienced an economic downturn.

Practice and In-Class Exercises

Note: Answers to all practice exercises can be found at the back of the book.

Exercise 25 (Practice)
Comma, Colon, and Semicolon Usage

Insert commas, colons or semicolons as appropriate:

1. The following furniture was ordered two tables three desks four chairs and four printers.

2. In order to graduate all students are required to complete courses in English, mathematics, accounting, and computer science.

3. This drawer contains basic office supplies letterhead envelopes printer paper stamps and a stapler.

4. Only four people failed to attend the sales meeting Paula Jacobs, Stan Martin, Georgia Gibson, and Monica Rodgers.

5. Please tell Marge that I will keep my 10:30 A.M. appointment however I will be unable to keep my 2:30 P.M. appointment.

Exercise 25 (In Class)

Comma, Colon, and Semicolon Usage

Insert commas, colons, or semicolons in the following sentences, as appropriate:

1. Our industry is capital intensive therefore fixed costs are unusually high.

2. She has a number of skills typing filing and word processing.

3. Please bring your latest printouts projections and graphics ideas to the meeting on Wednesday.

4. Do three things before you leave turn off all machines turn off all lights and sign out.

5. She did not like her job and her dislike of it was evident to all her coworkers.

6. Kay had no reason to go home early but she told us she could not stay.

7. Several people volunteered to arrive early to help set up the original committee members had backed out at the last minute.

8. Doug considered the plan a good one for two reasons it was financially sound and it would appeal to the company president, Mr. Jenkins.

9. Tim and Rob were competing for the same position the resulting tension in the department was obvious.

10. She complimented me several times on my work she told me that I had several good ideas.

PARENTHESES

Use parentheses to denote nonessential or supplementary information. The information contained within the parentheses could be one word or several paragraphs. If it is a complete sentence, do not put it in the middle of the text sentence.

Not Effective

We have several decisions (see page 4) to make regarding next year's budget.

Don't direct your reader to another part of your document in the middle of a sentence.

Effective

We have several decisions to make regarding next year's budget. (See page 4.)

Make your point first, then direct your reader elsewhere.

Not Effective

NASA oversees our space program.

Do not use abbreviations or acronyms without explaining them.

Effective

NASA (National Aeronautics and Space Administration) oversees our space program.

or

The National Aeronautics and Space Administration (NASA) oversees our space program.

Once you have spelled out the acronym, you can use the abbreviated form—*NASA*—in the remainder of the document.

Effective

Some of the most populous cities in the world (for example, New York, Paris, and London) are also among the most interesting.

Effective

Mr. Garver's recent article ("How to Plan for the 1990's") contains a great deal of information applicable to us.

The title is also considered an appositive and could be set off by commas instead of parentheses.

Punctuation of Parenthetical Material

When the parenthetical material is a complete sentence, begin the remark with a left parenthesis, then capital letter, period at the end, right parenthesis:

> The report enumerates several problems. (We should look at each of these problems carefully.)

> The details are given on page 14. (See Chapter 1.)

If the parenthetical material is not a complete sentence, punctuate according to grammatical structures it may contain which require punctuation.

> Teleconferencing (meetings via television), which is used more extensively now, can save us money.

No punctuation is required within the parentheses here, but be sure to set off the nonessential clause beginning with *which*—the parenthetical words don't change the need for proper punctuation in the rest of the sentence.

> Several people (including my manager, Marsha) attended the convention in Chicago.

Here a comma is required inside the parentheses because *Marsha* is an appositive. Normally an appositive is surrounded by commas, but the end parenthesis replaces the other comma here.

USE OF e.g., AND i.e.,

Often with parentheses two Latin phrases are used: *e.g.,* and *i.e. e.g.* means *for example* (exempli gratia). *i.e.* stands for *that is* (id est). *e.g.* is not used to denote an all-inclusive list—only an example. On the other hand, *i.e.,* for *that is,* is all-inclusive.

If you choose to use either Latin term, be sure you understand its meaning. If what you want to state is only a partial list or example, use *e.g.* If what you're adding is all-inclusive, use *i.e.* Be sure to follow the last letter *e* in either case with both a period *and* a comma. The correct format is:

> e.g.,   i.e.,

Use *e.g.,* if the issues you list are only *part* of what will be discussed.

> There are several issues to be discussed at the next staff meeting (*e.g.,* promotion, salary increases, and project reviews).

Use *i.e.,* if the three issues are all-inclusive; there are no other issues to discuss.

> Three issues will be discussed at the next staff meeting (*i.e.,* promotion, salary increases, and project reviews).

Practice and In-Class Exercises

Note: Answers to all practice exercises can be found at the back of the book.

Exercise 26 (Practice)

Parentheses

Correct the punctuation errors and any capitalization errors involved in parentheses usage in the following sentences. (Some sentences need no corrections.)

1. The projected figures are optimistic (see page 4).

2. His latest idea (to develop a new product this year) was received with skepticism.

3. We have held conferences in three major U.S. cities. (Los Angeles, New York, and Chicago)

4. The recent newspaper article ("The Latest in Computer Technology,") was mentioned at yesterday's meeting.

5. Someone from the IRS (Internal Revenue Service), called three times yesterday.

6. Sometime today you need to call Darren Wilson. (His phone number is in the book.)

Exercise 26 (In Class)
Parentheses

Correct the punctuation errors and any capitalization errors involved in parentheses usage in the following sentences. (Some sentences need no corrections.)

1. We want to tell you about our product (floor coverings.).

2. Several states (Texas, Delaware, and Oregon), would be ideal locations for another plant.

3. This new three-colored model (Made by Ivanex Corporation) is selling very well.

4. Maria, (the only experienced member of our staff) retired last month.

5. The cost of manufacturing our Model 2502 has increased by 10% in one year (See Appendix A for a full cost breakdown.)

6. Margaret deserved the promotion. (She has been with the company for more than ten years.)

UNDERLINING AND QUOTATION MARKS

Underline the titles of books, magazines, journals, and newspapers.

> The Wall Street Journal is a very informative publication.
>
> We should subscribe to Computer World.
>
> The San Jose News contains movie reviews every Friday.
>
> I saw Principles of Economics on her desk.
>
> Put in quotation marks the titles of chapters of books or articles from magazines, journal names, newspaper names, and seminar titles.
>
> "How to Deal with Office Politics" appeared in this month's issue of Fortune.
>
> An excellent article entitled "The Pre-Product Life Cycle" appeared in the current issue of Marketing Quarterly.
>
> Ten people from our department attended the seminar, "How to Deal with Difficult People."

Note: If the word merely describes the subject of an article or book, do not put quotation marks around the word:

> An excellent article on supervision appeared in the May issue.

Use quotation marks around a word or phrase to denote special use:

> Expressions of courtesy include "Thank you," "Please," and "You're Welcome."
>
> Many people find it difficult to distinguish between "affect" and "effect."
>
> His "lunch" consisted of a coke and a stick of gum.

Note that when the end quote mark appears at the end of a sentence, *the period always goes inside the end quote mark*. This rule also applies to the comma as well.

Practice and In-Class Exercises

Note: Answers to all practice exercises can be found at the back of the book.

Exercise 27 (Practice)
Underlining and Quotation Marks

Underline titles of books, magazines, and journals; put quotation marks around article titles in magazines or journals and chapter titles in books. Also put in quotation marks a word or words you want to use in a special way, or call special attention to.

1. The San Jose News interviewed several high-tech company presidents in last Monday's edition.

2. I have been subscribing to PC World for two years.

3. I read three times Understanding Difficult People in this month's issue of Psychology Today.

4. Since it was my job to write the new policy, I studied carefully the article entitled How to Write Effective Policies and Procedures.

5. A summary of the book was presented in The New York Times, The Los Angeles Herald, and the San Francisco Chronicle.

6. Many people misspell accommodate.

7. The article on computer technology for the '90s was discussed at Wednesday's department meeting.

Exercise 27 (In Class)

Underlining and Quotation Marks

Underline titles of books, magazines, and journals; put quotation marks around article titles in magazines or journals and chapter titles in books. Also put in quotation marks a word or words you want to use in a special way, or call special attention to. Some sentences are correctly punctuated.

1. We found appropriate ideas in Technology Today, PC World, and Computer Age.

2. The chapter entitled Politics in the Workplace seemed particularly important.

3. I suggested she read one of my favorite books How to Work for Difficult People.

4. Since she has been interested in jogging for two years now, I gave her a subscription to Runner's World for her birthday.

5. My manager suggested I review the chapter Comma Usage before I write another report.

6. My manager suggested I review the chapter on comma usage before I write another report.

7. Principal and principle are difficult words to use correctly.

8. Terry's recent report on marketing innovations was printed and distributed to all mid-level managers.

APOSTROPHE USAGE
TO FORM THE POSSESSIVE

The apostrophe in English is applied to certain words to show the concept of ownership or special relationship. We also call this situation the *possessive*. We have no difficulty applying the possessive when speaking. We know to put an *s* sound on certain words. We know that it is wrong to say "Marsha coat." We also know to include an *s* on these words when writing, but we are often uncertain about where to put the apostrophe. Today, to make matters worse, many people are unaware that an apostrophe is needed at all, or are so uncertain about where to put it that they leave it out altogether.

The apostrophe is not an optional mark of punctuation. It is required in certain cases. **Where** it is placed in the word is also critical. In all but a few situations, **'s** denotes what is called the *singular possessive,* or singular ownership—one person owns the thing or a single thing possesses the special relationship to the second noun. **s'** in almost every situation denotes *plural ownership;* that is, two or more people or things possess or have a special relationship to the second noun. **Where** the apostrophe is placed, then, is critical to proper understanding of the sentence.

First, let's look at how to tell when an apostrophe is needed at all. Two rules about English may help you here:

1. Every *s* word that needs an apostrophe can be turned into an *of* phrase:

    Karen's report—the report of (belonging to) Karen

    my manager's suggestion—the suggestion of my manager

    this year's figures—the figures of this year

    our employees' needs—the needs of our employees

If you can see the *of* phrase, this recognition will help you see the need for the apostrophe. If you can't readily see how "my manager's suggestion" can be reworded to "the suggestion of my manager," try the second approach.

2. Normally in English, two nouns rarely appear side by side in a sentence. When the first noun ends in *s,* that noun will almost always require the apostrophe. In most instances, the idea of possession is obvious: "my manager's desk." In other instances, the idea of possession or special relationship is difficult to see: "a minute's delay." In cases where the idea of ownership can't be readily seen, use the two-nouns-in-a-row rule to help you see the need for the apostrophe on the first noun.

There are a few exceptions to the preceding rule requiring an apostrophe on the first of two nouns when the first noun ends in *s:* "sales quota" does not require the apostrophe on *sales.* Perhaps at one time it did. In most other instances, an apostrophe will be required on the first noun.

Once you have determined that an apostrophe is needed, the second step is to determine **where** the apostrophe should be placed. In English, the apostrophe is either placed before the *s* to show what we call *singular possessive* or after the *s* to show the idea of *plural possessive.* We must determine how many of the things we are talking about. To determine the answer to that question, look at **only** the first of the two nouns. **Do not concern yourself with the second noun at all.**

Deborahs remarks

We know from Rules 1 and 2 that an apostrophe is needed on *Deborahs.* We have a hidden *of* phrase that shows ownership—"the remarks of Deborah." We also have two nouns in a row with the first one ending in *s.* The second noun also ends in *s,* but this noun is irrelevant. Remember, look **only** at the first noun to determine where to put the apostrophe. Ask yourself, "How many Deborahs do we have—one or more than one?" If you have only one, the proper placement of the apostrophe is before the *s.* If you have more than one of the first noun, place the apostrophe after the *s.* The correct placement in this case would be:

Deborah's remarks

Let's take another example:

the employees concerns

Here, again, we have a hidden *of* phrase: "the concerns of the employee/s." We also have two nouns in a row, with the first one ending in *s.* The second noun *(concerns)* also ends in *s,* but this noun is irrelevant. Where do we place the apostrophe on *employees?* Ask yourself how many employees we are talking about.

Here is a situation where your understanding of apostrophe usage is critical to the reader's being able to understand the sentence. Do you mean that one employee has concerns, or do you mean that several employees have concerns? Only you, the writer, know the answer to that.

If you mean that one employee has concerns, place the apostrophe in the singular form, like this:

the employee's concerns

If you mean that more than one employee has concerns, place the apostrophe in the plural possessive form, like this:

the employees' concerns

Again, the placement of the apostrophe has nothing to do with the noun *concerns*, only with the word *employees*.

Irregular Nouns

Accurate spelling of the singular possessive is usually quite easy. Spelling of the plural possessive, however, can sometimes cause problems. You must first be able to spell correctly the simple plural of the noun before you can form the plural possessive. English has, unfortunately, a few nouns whose plurals are not formed by simply adding *s*. Likely exceptions are those nouns whose singular forms end in *y, o,* and *f*. The plurals of the very unlikely irregulars —formed from nouns such as *man, woman,* and *child*—simply must be memorized. When you are unsure of a plural spelling, consult a dictionary. The plural form is always spelled out for irregular nouns.

Here are some irregular nouns, their singular possessive forms, their plural forms, and their plural possessive forms:

Singular	Singular Possessive	Plural	Plural Possessive
company	company's	companies	companies'
facility	facility's	facilities	facilities'
authority	authority's	authorities	authorities'
shelf	shelf's	shelves	shelves'
man	man's	men*	men's
woman	woman's	women*	women's
child	child's	children*	children's

*Notice that these plurals do **not** end in *s*. The plural possessive of these nouns is formed **very** differently than for most other nouns.

Proper Names That End in S

How do we form the possessive of people's names that already end in *s*—Jones, Reynolds, Hopkins, etc? The rule is , if the name is one syllable, we add **'s** to the name: "Mr. Jones's office"; however, "Mr. Jones' office" is also acceptable.

If the name is more than one syllable—*Reynolds, Hopkins,*—place the apostrophe after the *s*:

Darcy Reynolds' attendance record

Ms. Hopkins' suggestions

Be sure that you do not write "Mr. Jone's office" or "Darcy Reynold's attendance records" or "Ms. Hopkin's suggestions." To place the apostrophe before the *s* here means that their names are *Jone, Reynold,* and *Hopkin.*

The following are several examples of sentences that require the apostrophe to show possession:

People are finding themselves under more stress than ever, given *today's* busy lifestyle.

Today's busy lifestyle requires an apostrophe. Although it appears that we don't have two nouns side by side, we really do—*busy* is just an adjective modifying the noun *lifestyle.*

Therefore, we must turn *today* into an adjective by making it possessive (adding the apostrophe). Is it made possessive in the singular form—*today's*— or plural form—*todays'* ? *Today* denotes one day, so the *'s* form is always the correct form when *today's* appears before another noun.)

Can I please have *everyone's* cooperation?

The possessive of *everyone* is **always** *everyone's. Everyone* is called an indefinite pronoun. It is **always** singular, so this is the only form possible when making this word possessive—everyone's. Always put the word in the singular possessive form when it appears before another noun—even if the other noun is plural.

During a speech, it is important to keep the *audience's* attention.

Audience and *attention* are both nouns; audience is made possessive in the singular form because *audience* is thought of as a single group or single unit of people. An *of* phrase could also be formed from these words—During a speech, it is important to keep the attention **of the audience.** Whenever you can put the words into an *of phrase,* the possessive is required if you've omitted the *of* and re-ordered the words.

He did two *weeks'* work in two days.

Weeks and *work* are both nouns; make the first one possessive to create an adjective. *Weeks* is plural here because the sentence is talking about *two* weeks, which is more than one. So you must form the possessive on the plural spelling of the word—*weeks*—not on its singular form—*week*.

There will be 15 *minutes'* delay before we can start the meeting.

Minutes and *delay* are both nouns. Make the possessive on *minutes* to create an adjective. You can also easily turn this construction into an *of phrase*— There will be a delay **of 15 minutes**, so the possessive is needed if you re-order the words. To tell whether the apostrophe should be placed before the *s* (showing singular) or after the *s* (showing plural), ask yourself how many minutes the sentence is talking about. More than one minute? If so, the **plural possessive** is required—*minutes'*. Since the sentence mentions 15 minutes, which is more than 1, the plural possessive is required.

Sam took three *weeks'* vacation this year.

Weeks and *vacation* are both nouns, so the possessive is required on *weeks*. To determine whether to put the apostrophe before the *s* (which would show singular) or after the *s* (which would show plural), ask yourself how many weeks the sentence is referring to. Since the sentence mentions *three,* it's a case requiring the plural form—*weeks'*

We had an *hour's* delay before takeoff.

Possession is difficult to see in this sentence. However, **hour** and *delay* are both nouns, so the possessive is required on **hour.** How many hours is the sentence talking about? Only one, which you can see by the use of *an,* which is singular. We need, then, in this case, the singular form of the possessive, — *hour's*. Another test for needing *'s* on *hour* is to see if you have an *of phrase* hiding here, which you do: "We had a delay *of an hour* before takeoff." If you omit the *of* and reorder the words, the possessive form is required.

The *restaurant's* menu was reprinted last week.

Normally the possessive isn't used with inanimate objects, but, technically, to do so isn't grammatically wrong. Since **restaurant** and *menu* are both nouns, the possessive is needed on **restaurant**. As we speak this sentence, we naturally add the *s* to **restaurant**, but how is it punctuated? How many restaurants is the sentence speaking of? One, although *the* is often used in English before singular and plural nouns. We have to assume that each restaurant has its own menu. Since the context here requires the singular form, the possessive of **restaurant** will be *restaurant's*.

My *manager's* suggestions are always helpful.

Manager and *suggestions* are both nouns; the possessive is, therefore, required on **manager**. Ownership or possession is also easy to see here—the suggestions belong to my manager. If we were to speak this sentence instead of write it, we would automatically put the *s* on **manager**. But how is it punctuated if we were to write the same sentence? **Manager** requires the possessive because of the *two-nouns-in-a-row* rule. It is safe to assume that the writer has only one manager; therefore, **manager** should be put in the **singular possessive** form—**manager's**. The decision has nothing to do with the fact that *suggestions* is plural.

The *men's* coats are in the hall.

Here is a plural form of an irregular noun—*man*. The plural of *man* is not *mans,* but *men*.

Deborah's long-term decision is to stay with the company.

Even though this structure is slightly different, we still have two nouns in a row—ignore any intervening adjectives. It's still *Deborah's decision*.

Seven of our *company's* faithful and devoted employees retired this month.

Another variation—noun, adjective, coordinating conjunction, adjective, noun. Despite the intervening words, we still consider this structure to be two nouns in a row—*company's employees*.

We have three *years'* worth of data.

Any construction involving *worth of* usually requires the possessive on the preceding word. Either the singular possessive or the plural possessive could be required, depending on how many are being talked about:

A minute's worth of data.

Two months' worth of evidence.

Yours, Hers, Ours, Theirs

Remember that when writing **yours, hers, ours,** and **theirs,** *do not* put an apostrophe before the *s*. These pronouns are *already* in the possessive form:

The choice is yours.
Never *your's* or *yours'*.

The decision to change the marketing strategy will be hers.
Never *her's* or *hers'*.

Ours is an excellent report.
Never *our's* or *ours'*

The desks and file cabinets are theirs.
Never *their's* or *theirs'*

APOSTROPHE USAGE TO FORM CONTRACTIONS

The apostrophe is also used to form what are called **contractions**. A contraction is created when two words are combined into one by leaving out one or more letters. The apostrophe is placed where the missing letters would have been, had the words been spelled out. This form is usually not used in formal writing but is used extensively in conversation and in informal writing.

The following is a list of some of the most common contractions:

we are—we're

you are—you're

I am—I'm

The apostrophe denotes the missing *a*.

could have—could've

should have—should've

The apostrophe denotes the missing *h* and *a*.

who is—who's

it is—it's

he is—he's

The apostrophe denotes the missing *i*.

is not—isn't

can not—can't

do not—don't

did not—didn't

were not—weren't

could not—couldn't

will not—won't

The apostrophe denotes the missing *o*.

Could Have/Should Have

Many students misspell the contracted forms of **could have** and **should have**. They tend to spell them the way they sound when pronounced: *could of* and *should of*. These spellings are incorrect. Although both *should* and *of* are words and are spelled correctly here, the use of them together is wrong. *Of* is a preposition. What is needed is another helping verb to go with *should,* not a preposition. When in doubt, don't attempt the contraction—just write out *could have* or *should have*.

MOST COMMON CONTRACTION ERRORS

The biggest difficulties with contractions are with *its / it's,* w*hose / who's, your / you're,* and *their / they're / there.*:

Its/It's

Its is the possessive form of *it* and means *whose.*

It's is a contraction of *it is.*

> The company had (it's/its) books audited last month.

If you're not sure which form to use, substitute *it is* (for *it's*) and see if that sounds right: The company had **it is** books audited last month. Obviously, that form won't work here. So the correct form is *its.* The possessive is required here, meaning, whose books?

The sentence should read:

> The company had **its** books audited last month.

> It's/Its too soon to tell whether Mr. Sawyer will like our idea.

Substitute *it is* at the beginning and see if the words make sense—

> **It is** too soon to tell whether Mr. Sawyer will like our idea.

Yes, the construction sounds right, so the correct choice is *It's.*

> **It's** too soon to tell whether Mr. Sawyer will....

Whose/Who's

Whose is the possessive and normally used before a noun.

Who's is the contraction for *who is.*

Since **who's** is a contraction for *who is,* substitute *who is* in any sentence requiring one of these two spellings, and the correct choice becomes quickly obvious.

> I don't know whose/who's calculator this is.

Substitute **who is**: I don't know **who is** calculator this is. Obviously, this construction sounds wrong, so *whose* is the correct form:

I don't know **whose** calculator this is.

Whose/Who's going to attend the departmental meeting?

Substitute *who is*: Who is going to attend the departmental meeting? This construction sounds right, so use *who's*.

Who's going to attend the departmental meeting?

Your/You're

Your is the possessive always appearing before a noun.

You're is the contraction of *you are*.

Apply the same test in sentences requiring *your/you're* choices. Since *you're* is a contraction for *you are,* substitute *you are* in the appropriate place in the sentence, and see if it makes sense:

Let me know if your/you're going to the staff meeting.

Is it, "Let me know if **you are** going to the staff meeting..?" The substitution sounds right, so *you're* is the correct choice.

I have not read your/you're report yet.

Is it, "I have not read **you are** report yet...?" No. That sounds very wrong; therefore, the correct choice is *your*.

Their/They're/There

Their means *belonging to*:

Supermarkets will often emphasize **their** private labels.

They're is a contraction of *they are*:

They're attempting to increase sales with this approach.

There can be either a filler word with no particular meaning or an adverb meaning *where:*

There may be a good reason for this strategy. [Filler word]

The clerks placed today's orders **there** on the desk. [Adverb]

Practice and In-Class Exercises

Note: Answers to all practice exercises can be found at the back of the book.

Exercise 28 (Practice)
Apostrophe Usage

Make possessive (if necessary) the word in parentheses.

1. Who the new manager will be is (anybodys) guess.

2. For (everyones) health, please smoke only in designated areas.

3. There will be an (hours) delay before we can start.

4. I got a bonus equal to three (weeks) salary.

5. The explanation took ten (minutes).

6. Our (companys) policy is to require a college degree of all those interested in management.

7. The report is not on my desk; it may be on Mr. (Reynolds).

8. The (mens) coats are in the conference room.

9. We have not heard from them in two (weeks).

10. That (companys) policies need updating.

11. Thanks for filling in for Gladys with just an (hours) notice.

12. The two (clerks) mistakes cost the company a great deal of money to correct.

13. This (firms) finances are in good shape.

14. My (managers) personality could use some improvement.

15. (Johns) solution to the production problem proved effective.

16. Her (managers) opinion was that we should move ahead with the project anyway.

17. At the Tuesday staff meeting, it was agreed that new (couches) should be purchased for the (womens) lounge.

18. Several (businesses) will benefit from the recession.

19. The (computers) memory capacity is not large.

20. All of the (clerks) salaries were raised last month.

21. (Its) not a good idea to tell your manager how to do his/her job.

22. Don't judge a book by (its) cover.

23. (Who's/Whose) turn is it to make coffee?

24. I need to know (who's/whose) coming to the meeting.

25. Good salespeople are already motivated to sell; compensation and incentives merely direct (there/ their/ they're) efforts.

26. The shipment is on (its) way.

27. (Your/You're) performance appraisal is scheduled for today.

28. Debra told me that she thinks (your/you're) a person with a lot of good ideas.

29. (Its) not important (who's/whose) fault it is.

30. (You're/Your) report needs more specifics; (its) too general.

31. My suggestions are never taken as seriously as (Jims).

32. (There/their/they're) could be many benefits to such an aggressive financial plan.

33. The most successful (company's/companies'/ companies) will be those that are committed to and creative in responding early to human resource issues.

34. The company reevaluated (its) long-range plans for expansion.

35. The fund-raising letter is a good idea: was the idea (yours) or (hers)?

Exercise 28 (In Class)
Apostrophe Usage

Make possessive (if necessary) the word in parentheses.

1. My (managers) secretary went home early today.

2. The changes you suggest will cause a (months) delay in production.

3. Our estimate of (salaries) over the coming three (years) assumes no change during the first year.

4. In the past year, Barney has had three (managers).

5. When interviewing for a job, (ones) mannerisms are usually carefully noted by the interviewer.

6. I have three (weeks) vacation coming this year.

7. This (administrations) (policies) are difficult to understand.

8. The (presidents) speech was entertaining, although I had difficulty determining (its) relevance to our group.

9. All of the (supervisors) affected by the change attended (yesterdays) emergency meeting.

10. Most (managers) do not spell out to a new employee a comprehensive picture of working (conditions).

11. (Your/You're) right about that; we could use more help.

12. Advertising should appeal to all (buyers) good judgment.

13. My first reaction was that (Kirks) friend was joking.

14. Anything you propose will probably work, as long as you can present good (reasons) for justifying your idea.

15. Do you want to hire someone who will double (sales)?

16. The idea wasn't mine; maybe it was (Ms. Hopkins).

17. An (employees) incompetence is rarely the reason for conflict in the workplace.

18. We work in an industry where (there/their/they're) is little opportunity to differentiate ourselves from our competitors.

19. Do not give contradictory (answers) to (employees); be sure to tell each person the same thing.

20. I have just completed six (months) negotiations on an order that means a huge commission check for me.

21. I have often worked for (managers) who were definitely "take-charge" (individuals).

22. For (everyones) safety, please keep this door locked.

23. Many (managers) thrive on solving (crises).

24. Some managers are disorganized and can't manage their own time, much less anyone (elses).

25. Market research has shown that (there/their/they're) are 9 million high-potential customers.

26. How many (promotions) have you had in the last five (years)?

27. The spilled coffee marred the (tables) surface.

28. The (effects) of the last-minute change will not be known for several (weeks).

29. On a (moments) notice, good negotiators can change their strategy.

30. Sales people who maximize (there/their/they're) income will, at the same time, meet company objectives.

31. Getting ahead with many (bosses) means paying attention to their definition of "doing a good job."

32. James considered carefully the (staffs) (comments) about the new (policies).

33. Since the vice-president was going to be delayed, I had an (hours) reprieve before I had to give my presentation.

34. By restructuring some of our (company's/companies'/companies) policies, our turnover rate can likely be reduced.

35. Is this telephone number (yours)?

HYPHENATION

The hyphen (-) is used in two ways: (1) to connect separate words that form one adjective before a noun and (2) to divide a word at the end of a line when space will not permit printing the entire word.

Here are several two-, three-, and four-word adjectives which should be hyphenated to show that they form one adjective. Hyphenating words that form one thought visually helps your reader absorb the information faster.

> up-to-the-minute report
>
> last-minute preparation
>
> state-of-the-art technology
>
> a three-foot desk
>
> a four-year contract
>
> a five-mile walk
>
> a first-class job
>
> a high-grade copier
>
> two 7-pound weights
>
> 6 one-story buildings
>
> easy-to-use software
>
> off-the-record conversation
>
> all-powerful person
>
> coin-operated machine
>
> never-say-die attitude
>
> our much-discussed theories

Use a hyphen after each initial element in a series of compound modifiers with the same final element:

> We invested in several two- and three-bedroom houses.

Two goes with *bedroom*. But to avoid writing *bedroom* too many times, it is used only once, at the end. You must, however, show the proper connection to *bedroom* by using the hyphen after *two*.)

> We have several four-, six-, and eight-cylinder automobiles for sale.

Four, six, and *eight* all go with *cylinder*. But to avoid having to write *cylinder* three times, use it only once, at the end, but connect the adjectives to it with hyphens. Also be sure to put commas after the numbers, since these words are adjectives in a series as well.

Practice and In-Class Exercises

Note: Answers to all practice exercises can be found at the back of the book.

Exercise 29 (Practice)
Hyphenation

Add hyphens where appropriate to show that two or more words are considered *one* adjective.

1. My supervisor said I submitted a first class report.

2. Our state of the art technology interests many engineers.

3. Several high level managers attended the conference in Dallas.

4. He does many things that are considered self serving behavior.

5. The one step process is a big improvement.

6. She has been a long time employee of the firm.

7. He made me a take it or leave it offer.

8. We all work a ten hour day.

9. He has submitted several award winning ideas.

10. He always wears color coordinated neckties.

11. The standards will be phased in over a two to five year period, beginning January 1994.

12. The ten page report will include several assumptions about our competitors.

13. There will be a one hour delay before the shipment leaves.

14. Our four month contract expires in January.

15. I don't like face to face confrontations.

16. The 12 person committee met yesterday to consider necessary changes.

17. The Denver based company has been very successful.

18. He wanted us to take a do it yourself approach to the product literature.

19. The much needed refurbishing of the lobby was done last year.

20. He had a great deal of on the job training.

21. We would have a one time cost of $56,000.

Exercise 29 (In Class)
Hyphenation

Add hyphens where appropriate to show that two or more words are considered *one* adjective.

1. Our high style and high profile image perceived by potential customers is partly due to our advertising.

2. Rosalind's run of the mill designs didn't impress anyone.

3. It turned out to be a short lived solution.

4. I asked a simple question, but he insisted on giving me a ten minute answer.

5. A 40 hour week is not possible for individuals seeking management positions.

6. A meet the competition tactic is being employed by the other division.

7. I am glad that I work for a solution oriented manager.

8. The attention getting remark offended several people.

9. Employees often don't receive clear cut standards to follow.

10. The marketing department is responsible for meeting all agreed upon deadlines.

11. He offered all of them a more than fair solution.

12. The efficiency increasing procedure was praised by upper level management.

13. There's a company wide hiring freeze on right now.

14. In companies that use a five point appraisal scale, some managers sidestep the whole issue and rank everyone a "three."

15. Good communication is a two way process.

16. He values his ten year commitment to the company.

17. The success of our four state market plan will be difficult to judge during the first year.

18. When you're in charge, always try to run results oriented meetings.

19. The three piece suit is very popular at our company.

20. Two thirds of our employees favor the idea of flextime.

21. The five year average growth rate is approximately 13.2%, compared to 11.3% for all industries.

22. We may want to consider incentive based compensation.

23. The economy is slowing down, as seen in the most recent 12 month period.

CAPITALIZATION

Certain words in English begin with a capital letter wherever they occur in the sentence.

1. ***Capitalize names of companies, departments, organizations, and institutions.***

   Columbia University Sociology Department

   Clark Library Admissions and Records Office

   Kiwanis Club Planning Department

   Hunt-Wesson Foods Accounting Department

   TLX Corporation

2. ***Capitalize brand names.***

Macintosh personal computer	Rolex watch
Mitsubishi cellular phones	Hewlett-Packard calculator
Personal LaserWriter LS	Hallmark card

3. ***Capitalize a professional title when it is used with the person's name.***

Professor John Reinhold	John Reinhold, Professor
President Beth Bravero	Beth Bravero, President
Treasurer Lydia Dominguez	Lydia Dominguez, Treasurer

4. ***Capitalize the names of races, languages, nationalities, and the adjectives derived from them.***

Europe	European	England	English
Mexico	Mexican	Italy	Italian
America	American	France	French

5. ***Capitalize the names of historical events, periods, and policies.***

<table>
<tr><td>Reagan Era</td><td>The Depression of the Thirties</td></tr>
<tr><td>World War I</td><td>The Fifties</td></tr>
<tr><td>Vietnam War</td><td>Constitution of the United States</td></tr>
<tr><td>Civil War</td><td>Bill of Rights</td></tr>
<tr><td>Sick Leave Policy</td><td></td></tr>
</table>

6. ***Capitalize holidays, days of the week, and months of the year.***

<table>
<tr><td>Fourth of July</td><td>September</td></tr>
<tr><td>Christmas Day</td><td>Flag Day</td></tr>
<tr><td>Thanksgiving Day</td><td>Easter Sunday</td></tr>
<tr><td>Thursday</td><td>Labor Day</td></tr>
</table>

Do not capitalize seasons of the year unless the word begins the sentence:

We are planning to introduce a new line of sportswear this **fall**.

We had several new applicants this **spring**.

Summer is a good time to begin the interior renovation.

Absences seem to increase in the **winter** months.

7. ***Capitalize specific course names, lecture and seminar titles, but not general subject areas.***

All students should have taken **F**inite **M**ath.

All students should have taken **M**ath 201.

We are suggesting that our new managers take our recently developed course, *"Supervising Others."*

Notice that the title is also put in quotation marks.

All marketing personnel should have taken a class in statistics.

No capitalization is needed here because *statistics* is a general area of study.

All marketing personnel should have taken the course *Applied Statistics for Marketing.*

8. *Capitalize the titles of magazines, journals, and books; also capitalize chapter titles within books and article titles within journals and magazines.*

Capitalization rule for words within a title: the following classes of words are **not** capitalized:

1. small prepositions such as *to, for, of,* and *by;*

2. the articles *a, an,* and *the;*

3. the *to* of an infinitive;

4. short conjunctions—*or, but, and, so.*

Corporate Responsibility in the 90's.

Cost Effectiveness of Direct Mail Advertising

A Low-Cost Method to Reduce Energy Use.

The Need for Graphics Software.

The only exception to the preceding rule is if one of these words is the first word in the title. The first word in a title is **always** capitalized, no matter what the word is.

And Justice for All

Of Human Bondage

A Guide to Better Business Management

We ordered 20 reprints of the recent article entitled "Problems in Group Writing," from the Journal of Professional Communication, June 1991.

If **The** is part of the actual name of a magazine, journal, or newspaper, be sure to capitalize it to show that it is part of the official title: The Wall Street Journal. This newspaper's name is The Wall Street Journal. It is **not** Wall Street Journal.

9. *Capitalize sums of money when spelled out for legal documents.*

Ninety-four Dollars and Sixty-five Cents

Twenty-two Thousand Dollars

10. ***Capitalize city and state names—use the postal zip code abbreviations when you do not want to spell out the state name.***

We opened another office in **D**enver, **C**olorado.

Send your order to Teltek, P.O. Box 794, Denver, CO.

All zip code abbreviations consist of two capital letters:

California—CA, Oregon—OR, Tennessee—TN, Washington—WA, etc.

11. ***Capitalize* north, south, east, *and* west *and the various combinations of compass directions when they denote specific locations. When they are used simply as directions, do not capitalize.***

We have test-marketed several new products in the **S**outh this year.
Specific location

The **N**orthwest offers several job opportunities.
Specific location

Drive north three miles, then drive west on Interstate 450 two miles.
Direction only

We will be refurbishing the north end of the building this year.
Direction only

Practice and In-Class Exercises

Note: Answers to all practice exercises can be found at the back of the book.

Exercise 30 (Practice)

Capitalization

Add capital letters where necessary. Some sentences are correct as written.

1. the chairperson of the committee is Jeremy Ross, vice president of finance.

2. The south side of the parking lot is being resurfaced today.

3. On monday morning, Mr. Cordasco will review the document with all department managers.

4. This instrument was originally invented by a french physician.

5. The standard ford bumper jack is a portable mechanism for raising the front or rear of a car.

6. All companies would like to see more communication courses offered at the local colleges.

7. The environmental protection agency has made a great deal of progress in that area since 1975.

8. Why don't you write to the consumer affairs department?

9. The forklift operator on each shift will direct people out of the building through the loading dock, should a fire occur.

10. Wang laboratories has been in business for over 30 years.

11. We have had sales problems in the south this quarter.

12. Our guest speaker is professor Robert Rodriguez from the accounting department at Windham College.

13. Company holidays do not include flag day.

14. Our invited guest had a great deal to say about the reagan era.

15. There was an interesting article on laser technology in last month's issue of <u>pc computing</u>.

16. Please make me a copy of the article, "trends in computing: applications for the '90s."

17. Our fall order didn't arrive until October 24.

18. TCX corporation currently has the majority of market share.

19. We took the visiting vice-president to a european restaurant for dinner.

20. I would like to order 20 copies of the book, <u>A guide to better business management.</u>

Exercise 30 (In Class)
Capitalization

Add capital letters where necessary. Some sentences are correct as written.

1. Disappointed with earlier in-house workshops, we have recently contracted with dunmire associates, a team of communications consultants, to design a results-oriented workshop.

2. The completed sales proposal is attached.

3. We received the contract from New England power and light company.

4. We are requiring that all supervisors and managers in the department take the in-house seminar, "How to manage time effectively."

5. The design phase of this project should be completed on schedule.

6. The enclosed article, "The job market for College Graduates" should provide some helpful suggestions.

7. We are working hard to solve our current problem of low employee morale.

8. All supervisors in your department have been scheduled to to take one of the three supervision courses.

9. Labor day is a company holiday.

10. We opened three new offices in the northwest this year.

11. Turn east at the next corner, then drive west two miles.

12. The accounting department returned three travel request forms this week without processing them.

13. Cindy selected a mexican theme for the banquet.

14. Sylvia Gonzales, president of Liberty international, inc., has been our guest speaker before.

15. We have hired three new graduates this summer from Columbia university.

16. In the 1990's, the work force will be the key to the ability of american corporations to compete successfully.

17. Most of our customers live in the northeast or on the west coast.

NUMBER USAGE

We use numbers so frequently in business writing that it is important to format them in a way that makes them easy to comprehend. To make the absorption of numbers quick and easy for your reader, use the following rules when including numbers in sentences:

1. *Use words for numbers one through ten and figures for larger numbers.*

   The seven new employees will attend the orientation meeting tomorrow.

   The contract called for 11 modifications.

2. *If the number begins the sentence, always spell it out.*

   Forty-two members joined the organization this year.

3. *If figures are required for some numbers (larger than ten) in the sentence, use figures for all similar uses of numbers in the same sentence.*

   This year we hired 12 programmers, 16 sales representatives, and 3 secretaries.

   Normally, *3* would have been spelled out to follow Rule 1.

4. *If two numbers modify the same noun, use figures for the larger amount and words for the smaller amount.*

   I asked my secretary to buy 500 twenty-five-cent stamps.

   The firm owns three $35,000 computers.

5. *Use cardinal numbers for dates (with or without the year).*

   The project will be completed on August 6. (**not** August 6th)

   We will hold our next meeting on September 10, 19__.

The July 23 meeting should be attended by all mid-level managers. (**not** July 23rd)

6. ***Express percentages with figures and the per cent sign.***

Our sales increased 25% in January.

The proposed expansion could result in a 10% annual growth in profit.

If the percentage is used at the beginning of a sentence, spell it out, as in Rule 2:

Twenty-two per cent of our employees missed at least one day of work in January.

7. ***Very large numbers should be formatted for quick comprehension:***

We made $35 million this year in revenue.

Our company employs 385,000 people.

If the number begins the sentence, it must be spelled out:

Three-thousand dollars is a lot of money for this equipment.

8. ***Format fractions normally as figures:***

Sales were 2 1/2 times greater this quarter than last quarter.

Sales were 2.5 times greater this quarter than last quarter.

Do **not** write out a fraction—it takes much too long to read:

Sales were two-and-one-half times greater this quarter than last quarter.

Practice and In-Class Exercises

Note: Answers to all practice exercises can be found at the back of the book.

Exercise 31 (Practice)
Number Usage

Select the better format for the numbers presented in each sentence.

1. (Twenty-six/26) of our new hires were given raises this year.

2. We received (seventeen/17) new orders this month.

3. (Eleven/11) people attended the meeting.

4. We gave awards to (twenty-four/24) supervisors, (twelve/12) group leads, and (four/4) managers.

5. We shipped (sixteen/16) of the (twenty-five/25) orders were shipped today.

6. We received (twenty-five/25) (five/5)-pound boxes yesterday.

7. We are expecting sales to increase (five per cent/5%) this quarter.

8. (Twenty-five per cent/25%) of our employees asked for vacations in June this year.

9. The conference was attended by (two hundred/200) of our sales force.

10. The meeting to discuss the contract changes will be held on (August 6th/August 6).

11. Last year, we lost ($500,000/500,000 dollars) on our repair business.

12. Revenues from the 230 line represent (four per cent/4%) of net sales.

Exercise 31 (In Class)

Number Usage

Select the better format for the numbers presented in each sentence.

1. The (September 23rd/September 23) meeting has been changed to (September 24th/September 24).

2. The truck left (fifteen/15) boxes on the receiving dock.

3. We received responses from (thirty-four/34) managers, (twenty-one/21) supervisors, and (three/3) vice-presidents.

4. We enlarged the office by (twenty-three per cent/23%).

5. This shipment includes (twelve/12) (ten/10)-pound boxes.

6. (Nineteen/19) employees called in sick today.

7. The department now employs (nine/9) accountants.

8. The Midwest and Pacific divisions represent (29 per cent/29%) of sales, but (34 per cent/34%) of total expenses.

9. We will hold a special meeting on (May 3/May 3rd) to address that issue.

10. We completed (five/5) (Thirty-five Thousand dollar/$35,000)contracts this quarter.

11. Because the A-15 filter has decreased overall engine wear by (twenty per cent/20%), it should be included as a standard item in all of our new models.

12. These industry and market trends demonstrate that a (thirty per cent/30%) growth rate may be an unrealistic target.

CONFUSING WORDS

The following words are some of the most commonly confused in business writing.

Accept/Except

Accept—agree to; receive; take willingly [verb]

> I am happy to accept your offer.
>
> I accept this gift with gratitude.
>
> I will not accept your proposal after July 1.

Except—with the exclusion of, all but [preposition]

> All the books except one have arrived.
>
> Everyone is present except Marion.
>
> I like all of your ideas except one.

Affect/Effect

Affect—to influence [verb]

> Your recent behavior will not affect my decision.
>
> The recent economic picture will probably affect the outcome.
>
> The opening of three new sales territories should affect sales for the better.

Effect—result [noun]

> The effects of the changes are not yet known.
>
> He made that comment for effect.

Effects—personal belongings [noun]

> She kept her personal effects locked in her desk.

Effect—to bring about [verb]—seldom used

> The new manager planned to effect many changes in the department.

Amount/Number

Amount—refers to items in bulk or mass

> The amount of land available in our area for industrial development is almost unlimited.
>
> The amount of work accomplished was impressive for the time that we had.

Number—refers to items that can be counted

The number of employees who are going to the picnic is 959.

We ordered a large number of new forms.

Criterion/Criteria

Criterion—a standard for judging (singular)
Criteria—standards for judging (plural)

He had only one criterion for success: cost savings.

He listed three criteria we have to meet.

Farther/Further

farther—refers to measurable, physical distance

The new office is farther from the downtown area than the old office was.

Portland is farther from Los Angeles than Dallas is.

further—use in all other cases

I do not want to discuss this situation any further.

If you need further help, see me.

Fewer/Less

fewer—use with nouns that can be counted

We had *fewer defects* in this month's production than last month's.

Fewer employees left the company this year than last year.

less—use with nouns that can't be counted

We had *less absenteeism* this month than last month.

I noted *less optimism* at this meeting than at the last meeting.

There was *less discussion* over this issue than over salary raises.

Moral/Morale

moral—right and proper conduct; ethical [adjective]

He seems to be a moral person.

I have a moral obligation to do my best.

morals—right and proper conduct [noun]

He is a person with high morals.

moral—the inner meaning of a story

The moral of the story is, "Don't count your chickens before they're hatched."

morale—prevailing mood and spirit

Office morale has never been higher.

Since Mr. Morgan took over, office morale has been low.

Personal/Personnel

personal—belonging to an individual

I keep my personal belongings in my desk.

My personal opinion is that Joe is a good worker.

personnel—group of workers or employees

All personnel need to report to work by 7:30 a.m. every day.

Your personnel file is on my desk.

The Personnel Department is in Room 225.

Principal/Principle

principal—a leader or head of a group [noun]

The principal and his assistant spoke with all concerned parents.

The principals *(major players* in a situation) met at the Hilton to discuss their options.

principal—main, chief [adjective]

The principal reason I cannot stay late is that the last commuter train leaves at 8:45 p.m.

My principal objection to the plan is that it doesn't allow us enough time to make the changes.

My principal objective is to become a manager by the time I am 35.

My principal concern is for office morale.

principal—lump sum of money plus interest to be paid in a bank loan [noun]

Principal and interest payments are due on the 30th of each month.

principle—rule or basic truth [noun]

He has one guiding principle: honesty.

From time to time, I refer to my old textbook, <u>Accounting Principles</u>.

He is a man of unswerving principles.

She understands well the principles of effective leadership.

Practice and In-Class Exercises

Note: Answers to all practice exercises can be found at the back of the book.

Exercise 32 (Practice)
Confusing Words

1. He does not like to (accept/except) new ideas.

2. Everyone attended the meeting (accept/except) me.

3. His decision (affected/effected) several people.

4. She removed all of her personal (affects/effects) from the desk.

5. We are hoping that he is a person who can rapidly (affect/effect) change.

6. David has asked us to look for the (affects/effects) of low office morale.

7. The (amount/number) of absences alarmed John.

8. The (amount/number) of decisions Bob has made since he took over is impressive.

9. The (amount/number) of criticism he received after the meeting was slight.

10. Our other building is located (farther/further) down this street.

11. I don't want to discuss the issues any (farther/further).

12. (Fewer/less) solutions were generated at this meeting than at last week's meeting.

13. Personnel received (fewer/less) applications for employment this June than last June.

14. He is a person of high (morals/morales).

15. The (moral/morale) of the story is "better safe than sorry."

16. Office (moral/morale) has definitely gone up since Steve took over.

17. He told me to take the papers to the (Personal/Personnel) office.

18. She brought no (personal/personnel) items to the office.

19. (Principal/Principle) and interest are due the first of every month.

20. He has run this company based on two guiding (principals/principles).

21. The lack of opportunity for advancement is my (principal/ principle) concern about taking this job.

22. His (principal/principle) objection to the plan is that its implementation is too costly.

23. She will be attending a seminar this week called "(Principals/Principles) of Effective Supervision."

24. Our team has spent several days discussing new (criterion/criteria) for product testing.

Exercise 32 (In Class)
Confusing Words

1. I (accept/except) your decision to leave the department.

2. All of the pages (accept/except) three have been typed.

3. I hoped that my argument would (affect/effect) my manager's decision to implement some new accounting procedures.

4. Her remarks seemed to have no (affect/effect) on Bill.

5. We are having difficulty assessing the (amount/number) of interest in the company picnic.

6. The (amount/number) of rejects has dropped significantly this week.

7. We are (farther/further) along on this project than I realized.

8. We need to walk five blocks (farther/further).

9. This report has five (fewer/less) pages than last month's report.

10. Many people have expressed (fewer/less) dissatisfaction with our new insurance carrier.

11. This decision requires a (moral/morale) choice.

12. Studies have shown that flextime improves employee (moral/morale).

13. All (personal/personnel) will get Friday off.

14. My (personal/personnel) opinion isn't worth much here.

15. Our (principal/principle) product sells well in the East.

16. I saw an interesting article on my manager's desk: "(Principals/Principles) of Effective Leadership."

17. The (principal/principle) and interest payments opn this equipment are quite high.

18. She follows one important (principal/principle) in her work: honesty.

19. Her (principal/principle) talent is negotiating.

20. The (principals/principles) met to discuss the contract.

21. In selecting the city for our new manufacturing site, which (criterion/criteria) is the most important—the cost of office space or the availability of skilled workers?

GLOSSARY OF GRAMMAR TERMS

Appositive

A word or group of words following a noun that describes the noun. An appositive does not contain a verb. An appositive can be essential information or nonessential information. To determine whether the word or group of words is/are essential, look at the noun the appositive describes. If the noun does not indicate *exactly* who or what is being referred to, the additional word or words will help to clarify. In that case, *do not* surround the appositive with commas. If, on the other hand, the subject (noun) is precise, the additional word or words **could** be omitted; hence, surround the word or words with commas to show it is/they are only supplementary information.

Apostrophe—possession

A mark (') used to indicate ownership or a special relationship to the noun that follows. To show ownership, we put an *s* and the apostrophe mark (') on the owner—noun, thus turning the owner into an adjective telling *whose?* If the owner is singular in number, we use the *'s* form to show ownership. If the owner is plural, we add *s'*. Irregular plurals are treated differently. *Ownership* is a very broad concept in English. Individuals can *own* things; groups can *own* things; places can *own* things; and inanimate objects can *own* things. Many statements we make about *time* are also put in the possessive to show a particular relationship to the noun next to it. Don't try to imagine ownership here. Just remember to use the apostrophe to denote certain time relationships. Example: "I took a week's vacation in June." If more than one week, we use the *s'* form to denote more than one: "I took three week**s'** vacation in June."

Apostrophe—contraction

A mark (') used to shorten a two-word construction to one word by leaving out one or more letters and adding the apostrophe where the omitted letter(s) would normally be. Commonly used contractions are *it's* for *it is, don't* for *do not,* and *you're* for *you are.* Do not confuse this usage of the apostrophe with the one used for possession.

Clause

A group of words with a subject and verb. Technically, a clause could be only two words—a noun (that serves as the subject) and a verb (action or linking) that make sense with the noun. *Table (subject) ran (verb)* makes no sense together; therefore, it is not a clause. The clause may also include phrases (a group of related words without a verb) and other nouns.

Clause, Adjective

A group of words containing a subject and verb but which begins with a word that makes the clause unable to stand alone as a sentence—most adjective clauses begin with *who, which,* or *that.* The *who, which,* or *that* often serves as the subject of the clause. These clauses always describe a noun somewhere else in the sentence and answer the question, which one/s? what kind? or how many? Example: "The stores **that remain open until 9 p.m.** appear to be more profitable." In this example, *that* serves as the subject of the clause. The independent clause subject is *stores* and independent clause verb is *appear.* The adjective clause answers the question, which stores?

Clause, Adverb

A group of words containing a subject and verb but which begins with a subordinate conjunction (e.g., *until, because, if,* and *since*). This beginning word, by its very nature, *subordinates* the thought expressed to a more important thought somewhere else in the sentence—either before the adverb clause or after it. "**If you need additional information concerning the findings on this issue,** please call me." Adverb clauses usually answer one of these questions—Why? How? When? or For what reason?

Clause, Independent or Main

A group of words containing a subject and verb. An independent or main clause, theoretically, could be only two words long—a noun (that serves as the subject) and verb (action or linking) that makes sense with the subject. A main clause (or independent clause) is the main idea in the sentence and can stand alone as a complete thought. The main clause **cannot** begin with a subordinate conjunction; otherwise, the clause is turned into a subordinate or dependent clause.

Clause, Noun

A group of words containing at least a subject and verb. The clause usually begins with *that.* Given the kind of thought a noun clause expresses, it cannot stand alone as an independent thought. Noun clauses answer the question, *What?* Example: "I told George **that he needed to set aside three hours for tomorrow's budget meeting.**" The noun clause answers the question, *What did I tell George?* The independent clause is *I told George.*

Clause, Subordinate

A group of words beginning with either a relative pronoun or subordinate conjunction followed by, at minimum, a subject (noun) and verb. There are three types of subordinate clauses—adverb, adjective, and noun. All three types contain a subject and verb but cannot stand alone as a main thought or independent clause because of the word that begins the clause. Adverb clauses begin with a subordinate conjunction such as *since, because, after,* etc. Adjective clauses begin usually with *who, which,* or *that*. Noun clauses usually begin with *that*.

Dangling Modifier

An introductory phrase not followed immediately by its logical subject. The introductory phrase can begin with an infinitive, a participle, or a preposition. Because a phrase has no subject, it is critical that the noun immediately following the phrase be the subject spoken of in the phrase. If the phrase is not followed by the correct noun or pronoun, the introductory phrase is called *dangling*—it has no logical reference in the sentence to connect to.

Even if you can understand what is meant, the construction is still logically incorrect. Example: "After discussing the issue at great length, the best strategy seemed to be to buy, not make, the necessary components." Here we have an introductory prepositional phrase followed by the noun *strategy*. (*The* and *best* are adjectives which are to be ignored in the analysis.) The assumption, due to the word order, is that the strategy had been discussing the issue. Obviously, this is an illogical connection.

To correct a dangling modifier, turn the introductory phrase into a dependent clause (thus adding a subject in the introductory part) OR leave the introductory phrase as is, but rearrange the word order of the independent clause following, so that the subject of the phrase is placed at the beginning of the clause.

Corrected: "After discussing the issue at great length, **we** concluded that the best strategy seemed to be to buy, not make, the necessary components."

Direct Object

A noun that usually answers, *What?* A direct object often follows the verb. "I like doughnuts." *Doughnuts* is a direct object, telling what I like.

Expletive

A filler word such as *it* and *there* not used as their regular parts of speech, and **not** the subject of the sentence: "It is difficult to know what to do." In this sentence *It* is a filler word—a way to get into the sentence—but **not** the subject of the sentence nor a pronoun standing for a noun. *It* here isn't standing for anything. Rewording the sentence makes this obvious: "To know what to do is difficult." With the rewording, the *it* is gone altogether, so *it* couldn't have been the sentence subject. You can't throw out the subject and still have the same meaning. *To know* [the infinitive] is the sentence subject.

There is another *filler* word—a way to get into the sentence: "There are several reasons why Joe left the company." *There* is merely a filler word here, not an adverb telling where. It is simply a way to get into the sentence, but *there* is not the sentence subject. Reword, it and *there* drops out: "Joe left the company for several reasons." The subject is *Joe*.

Gerund

An **-ing** verb form being used as a noun. It is one of the four *verbals* in English. Verbals look like verbs but are serving another function in the sentence—adjective, adverb, or noun. *A gerund is never the verb.* The gerund serves as either (1) the subject of the sentence, (2) a direct object after a verb telling *what,* or (3) an *-ing* noun in a prepositional phrase.

Hyphen

A mark (-) used to connect words together which form one adjective. The words *state-of-the-art* form one adjective and so are connected with hyphens to show that they should be read as a single descriptive idea. A hyphen is also used to divide a word when space is short at the end of a line.

Infinitive

To + verb root. The infinitive form is never used as the verb in the sentence but serves as either an adjective, noun, or adverb. Examples of infinitives: *to go, to consider, to walk,* and *to think.* It is one of the four types of verbals. As an adjective: "The person to contact to make proper arrangements is Mrs. Langley." The infinitive *to contact* is an adjective here that answers the question, *which person?* The verb is *is.*

Linking Adverb

A special kind of adverb used after an independent clause to join another independent clause to it, showing the relationship of the first thought to the second. Examples of linking adverbs are *moreover, nevertheless, however,* and *consequently.* Linking adverbs are preceded by a semicolon and followed by a comma when joining two independent clauses: "I prepared thoroughly for the presentation; nevertheless, I could have done more." When this same type of adverb is used in the middle of a single independent clause, the word functions merely as an unnecessary interruption and is termed, appropriately, an *interrupter.* In this case, the word is surrounded by commas to show that it could be omitted from the sentence: "I, nevertheless, prepared thoroughly for the presentation."

Parts of Speech

One of eight functions of words: (1) noun, (2) verb, (3) adjective, (4) adverb, (5) preposition, (6) pronoun, (7) conjunction, or (8) interjection. A word can serve as only one part of speech at a time. However, in a different sentence with a different context, the word might be used as a different part of speech. The word *since,* for example, can be either a subordinate conjunction or preposition, depending on what words follow it. The word *since* can't, however, be both a preposition and conjunction at the same time.

Participle, Past

The *-ed* past tense form of the verb preceded by *have, had, was, were, are, is,* and *am*. If one of these forms precedes the verb, the past participle is functioning as part of the verb phrase. If the past participle is **not** preceded by a form of *to have* or *to be,* the past participle is functioning as an **adjective**.

Do not confuse simple past tense with the past participle:

Our office building **was constructed** in the late 1800s.
Past participle—part of verb phrase.

The workmen **constructed** the building in 90 days.
Simple past tense—**not** a past participle.

Constructed in the late 1800s, our office building is not earthquake-safe.
Past participle as adjective—modifies *building*.

Note: most past participles end in *-ed*; however, irregular verb forms can occur—some past participles end in *t (built),n (torn),* and *d (paid)*.

Participle, Present

A present tense verb with an **-ing** ending. The present participle can be either (1) a noun (gerund); (2) part of the verb if preceded by *is, was, were, will be, shall have been,* etc.; or (3) an adjective, in which case the **-ing** verb form will stand alone—no *is, was,* etc. will precede the **-ing** word. As a gerund: "Talking on the phone is something I dislike." As part of the verb: "Debbie is talking on the phone." As an adjective, "Talking on the phone, Debbie motioned for me to come in."

Phrase

A group of related words without a verb. Phrases can be either gerund, infinitive, prepositional, or participial.

Phrase, Gerund

A phrase beginning with a gerund (an **-ing** verb form not preceded by a helping verb) that serves as the subject of the sentence, as a direct object telling *what,* or as a noun after a preposition. Examples: "Leaving early is frowned on by management." The gerund phrase which is also the subject of the sentence here is *Leaving early*. "Laura enjoys presenting proposals to senior management." Here, *presenting proposals to senior management* is a gerund phrase serving as a direct object, telling what Laura enjoys. "Before leaving the office, I put a copy of the meeting agenda on Phil's desk." Here, *Before leaving the office* is a gerund phrase within the prepositional phrase *before leaving the office*.

Phrase, Infinitive

To + verb root followed by other related words. "To work on Saturdays is something I detest." *To work on Saturdays* is the infinitive phrase and the subject of the sentence.

Phrase, Participial

An **-ing** verb not preceded by a *to be* or *to have* form followed by related words. The participial phrase always performs an adjective function, describing a noun either before or after it. Example: "Mr. Markham, leaving the office early, hurried to catch the bus." *Leaving the office early* is a participial phrase describing *Mr. Markham. Leaving* is not the verb of the sentence. The verb is *hurried*.

Another test for a participial phrase is that it can be moved to the other side of the word it describes: "Leaving the office early, Mr. Markham hurried to catch the bus."

Phrase, Prepositional

A group of words beginning with a preposition followed by other related words. The most common structure is *prep + noun* or *prep + adjective + noun*. A prepositional phrase, although it always contains a noun or pronoun, will never contain the subject of the sentence.

Pronoun/Antecedent Agreement

The agreement in number (singular or plural) and gender (male, female, neuter) between a pronoun and the noun it refers to.

"All **employees** should bring **their** ideas to the meeting." Since **employees** is plural, the pronoun referring to them must also be plural. We don't have to worry about gender here because the plural in English (*their*) is neither masculine nor feminine. However, the following sentence with a singular subject requires a singular pronoun, **his/her**: "Each **employee** should bring **his/her** ideas to the meeting."

Pronoun, Unclear Reference

The use of a pronoun without clear reference to a noun. The pronoun *this* in English is very overused as a stand-alone word. Using it alone often creates confusion for the reader: "My manager came to work early today and asked me to make his coffee. **This** irritated me." This what? His early arrival? His request that you make coffee? To be precise, always follow **this** with the noun it refers to: "My manager came to work early this morning and asked me to make his coffee. This request irritated me."

Sentence

At minimum, one noun (subject) and one verb. The thought conveyed must make sense and must be able to stand alone as an independent idea. A sentence can contain other words as well—adjectives, adverbs, prepositional phrases, subordinate clauses, etc.

Sentence Types

Determined by the number of independent and subordinate clauses a sentence contains. In business, the three most important types are (1) simple sentence, (2) compound sentence, and (3) complex sentence.

Sentence, Complex

Contains one independent clause and one subordinate clause, in either order. Example: "Since the figures have not arrived from Accounting, I cannot complete this section of the report." *or* "I cannot complete this section of the report since the figures have not arrived from Accounting."

Sentence, Compound

Contains two independent clauses, separated by either a semicolon or by a comma **and** coordinating conjunction. The compound sentence does not contain a subordinate clause. Example: "I want to do well; I also want to be promoted." **or** "I want to do well, **and** I want to be promoted."

Sentence Fragment

Created when the words in print contain a subject but no verb or a verb but no subject, yet the words are punctuated like a complete sentence. A fragment is also created by assuming a verbal is a verb: "Frank, leaving the office early on Friday to catch the 2:45 commute train." Everything beginning with *leaving* is part of a participial phrase describing Frank. *Leaving* is not the verb of the sentence; however, the words are punctuated as if they were a stand-alone thought or independent clause. To correct the fragment, add a verb: "Frank, leaving the office early on Friday to catch the 2:45 commute train, felt guilty."

Sentence, Simple

Contains only one independent clause—either a subject and verb, or two subjects and one verb, or one subject and two verbs. It may also contain phrases or other parts of speech. A simple sentence could contain many words, but only one independent clause.

Subject

The noun in the sentence that is logically connected to the verb. It is either the noun or pronoun doing the action described or is the noun or pronoun described with a linking verb.

Subject/Verb Agreement

Agreement in number and gender between the subject and verb of the sentence. If the subject is singular (only one of something or someone), the verb in the sentence must be in singular form: *Barbara studies...* (singular subject followed by singular form verb); however, *Barbara study* would be wrong. *Study* is the verb form used with *I* and *they*.

Verb, Action

Tells what the subject is doing or what happened or will happen to the subject. The verb always expresses action within a time frame: "The vice-president read our report on Thursday." Here *read* is a past-tense verb showing action. "Our report was read by the vice-president on Thursday." In this sentence, *was read* tells what happened to the report—the subject. Sometimes the subject can complete more than one action in a sentence: "Tom made 20 copies and distributed them before 4 p.m." This sentence contains two verbs because Tom did two things: *made* and *distributed*.

Verb, Auxiliary or Helping

Used with other verbs to create different shades of meaning. Some helping verbs include *will, would, can, must, should, could, may, and might*. Many can be combined with *been: should have been writing, could have been involved, must have been noticed, will be watching, would be attending,* etc. Other combinations include *may go, might enlist, should analyze, could promote,* etc.

Verb, Linking

A small class of verbs which do not express action but which serve to *link* the subject to either (1) a noun that *re-names* the subject in some way or (2) an adjective that describes the subject. The most common linking verb is a *to be* form: *was, were, is, will be,* etc. "My manager will be happy when she hears that we got the contract." *Manager* is linked to an adjective that describes her (*happy*) by the linking verb *will be*.

"Stephen Chui is our new manager." The subject *Stephen Chui* is linked to a noun that renames him (*manager*) by the linking verb *is*.

Other linking verbs include *appear, smell, taste, seems,* and *looks*. Of course, each of these linking verbs can take slightly different forms—*appeared, will appear, tasted, seemed,* and *looked*.

"Our performance this year looked impressive until July." The linking verb *looked* links the subject *performance* to an adjective that describes *performance—impressive*.

Answers to Practice Exercises

Exercise 1
Identifying Nouns
1. notes, conversation
2. manager, software
3. interest, balance
4. computers, time, use
5. literature, decision
6. years, distinction, fashion, campaigns
7. ideas, call
8. advantages, system
9. format, friendliness or user friendliness, design
10. type, account, plan

Exercise 2
Identifying Verbs
1. takes
2. can be (LV); can do (remove the adverb *not*)
3. will mail
4. read
5. sent *(to check out* is an infinitive, not a verb; a verb must express time—past, present, or future; *to check* does not express time, so it can't be a verb)
6. will ask
7. is (LV) *(to work* is an infinitive; see #5 above)
8. felt, was evaluating, walked
9. came, got (LV)
10. perform, take
11. has done
12. is
13. ignore, likes
14. was achieved
15. are (LV)
16. are assuming

Exercise 3
Identifying Adjectives
1. Our, pricing, the, several, internal, external
2. one
3. Increasing, the, price
4. much, the

5. a, stimulating, everyone's
6. the, an, articulate, dependable, personable
7. this, improved, safe, nonpolluting, durable
8. three, internal, workload, optimistic
9. further, a, definite
10. these, perfect, the, conference
11. the, attached, investment, the, first, six, the, fiscal
12. the, three, the, wrong
13. a, supreme
14. the, company-owned, computer, five
15. the, colorful, informative

Exercise 4
Identifying Adverbs
1. clearly
2. carefully, very
3. automatically
4. immediately, surely
5. not, easily, away
6. too
7. somewhat, nervously
8. already
9. exceptionally, well
10. scarcely
11. never
12. carefully
13. often
14. effectively, efficiently
15. completely
16. severely

Exercise 5
Identifying Pronouns
1. Anyone, me
2. He, me, we
3. none (*it* here is an expletive—a filler word—but doesn't really stand for a noun)
4. (You—understood)
5. I
6. None, he
7. He, us
8. none
9. Few, you
10. none (*it* is an expletive filler here)
11. I, her
12. We

13. none
14. most
15. he, he

Exercise 6

Identifying Prepositions

1. In 1990, of our production
2. of personnel files, beside his desk
3. in my office, by noon
4. for improvement, through proper channels
5. with the company, until July 30
6. over my manager's head, on this issue *(to go* is an infinitive)
7. of the report, of next year's sales projections
8. into Chicago, at noon, on Thursday
9. under the previous management, in a casual style
10. with your approval, from Mr. Henley
11. to the contract change, within three days *(to respond* is an infinitive)
12. of the information, in the hands, of our attorneys, in Chicago
13. for a few hours, for tomorrow's presentation
14. between you and me, with her new position
15. to the employee lunchroom

Exercise 7

Identifying Conjunctions

1. (sc) when (s) you (v) fulfill
2. (cc) and
3. (cc) and
4. (sc) although (s) I (v) have been
5. (sc) as (s) you (v) know
6. (sc) until (s) I (v) hear
7. (sc) if (s) changes (v) are
8. (sc) unless (s) business (v) improves
9. (sc) while (s) I (v) was walking
10. (sc) although (s) vacation (v) is
11. (cc) and
12. (cc) or
13. (cc) but
14. (sc) as soon as (s) projections (v) are
15. (cc) and *(since* is a preposition here)

Exercise 8

Identifying Adjective Clauses

1. that is parked—car (essential)
2. that arrived yesterday—bill (essential)
3. who won the prize—people (essential)
4. which is located on First Street—office (nonessential)

5. that is polluted—air (essential)
6. that came in after 5 p.m.—reports (essential)
7. who works hard—person (essential)
8. who has considerable experience in selling new product ideas—Donna Roberts (nonessential)
9. that prohibits smoking indoors—policy (essential)
10. which is scheduled for a July 1 completion—cafeteria (nonessential)
11. who has been with the company for 15 years—Gregory Delgado (nonessential)
12. that will impress your audience—way (essential)
13. that we need to consider—advantages and disadvantages (essential)
14. who is in charge of our Atlanta office—Jonathan Martin (nonessential)
15. that we will face—problems (nonessential)

Exercise 9

Distinguishing Between Types of Subordinate Clauses

1. **Even though** we did submit the report on time—adverb
2. **Unless our** market share increases—adverb
3. **that** would likely be implemented—adjective
4. **that** the company isn't currently hiring programmers—noun
5. **that** would improve office communications
6. **unless** the rain stops—adverb
7. **until** we become more efficient—adverb
8. **that** we would be getting new word processing software—noun
9. **that** two major design changes could cause significant problems—noun
10. **Although** I attempted to console Stephanie—adverb

Exercise 10

Identifying Infinitives

1. to identify, to recommend
2. to reach, to send
3. to demonstrate
4. to go
5. to persuade, to change
6. none
7. to use
8. to stimulate, to cut
9. to find
10. to ask
11. to think
12. to increase
13. to effect
14. to target
15. to ensure

Exercise 11
Identifying Gerunds
1. **Relocating** our Los Angeles plant—subject
2. of **offering** in-house seminars—noun in prepositional phrase
3. **Determining** the usefulness of the software—subject
4. **Winning**—subject
5. **writing**—noun after linking verb renaming subject *job*
6. **Detailing** your travel expenses—subject
7. **Maintaining** good customer relations—subject
8. **writing** software—direct object
9. His **reporting** of the facts—subject
10. by **flying** to New York on Friday—noun in prepositional phrase
11. for **including** these figures—noun in prepositional phrase
12. **Purchasing** new equipment—subject
13. **Checking** figures—subject; before **presenting**—noun in prepositional phrase
14. **Understanding** the client's needs—subject
15. of **following** your suggestions—noun in prepositional phrase

Exercise 12
Identifying Present Participles
1. is presenting—verb
2. Arriving (at work early)—adjective describing *I*
3. Addressing (the group)—adjective describing *Tim*
4. are sending out—verb; announcing (our new discount prices)—adjective describing *flyers*
5. working (rapidly)—adjective describing Joe and Sherry
6. had been speaking—verb
7. standing (before a large audience)—adjective describing *Dolores*
8. had been working—verb
9. Speaking (rapidly)—adjective describing *Jeff*
10. will be going—verb
11. has been preparing—verb
12. Running (to catch the shuttle bus)—adjective describing *I*
13. were operating—verb
14. signing (the contract)—adjective describing *Cliff*
15. is collecting—verb

Exercise 13
Identifying Past Participles
1. was blocked—verb
2. has taken—verb (irregular form)
3. have mentioned—verb (remove the adverb *consistently*)
4. received (early this morning)—adjective describing *shipment* was left—verb

5. had accomplished—verb
6. driven (by the desire to succeed)—adjective describing *Margaret*
7. had predicted—verb
8. typed (by Katherine)—adjective describing *report*
9. had concluded—verb
10. were shared—verb
11. have been mailed—verb
12. Completed (at today's meeting)—adjective describing *suggestions* were forwarded—verb
13. had completed—verb
14. none (*shipped* is simple past tense, no *to have/be* form in front of it)
15. used (by everyone in the department)—adjective describing *computer*
16. has been delayed—verb; requested by the customer—adjective describing *revisions*

Exercise 14
Identifying Participles and Gerunds
1. were supplied—past participle as verb
2. writing (a long report)—gerund as subject
3. has created—past participle as verb
4. were given—past participle as verb
5. working (without a break)—present participle as adjective describing *we*
6. (before) ordering—gerund in prepositional phrase
7. Walking to the office—present participle as adjective describing *he*
8. speaking (to the new hires)—pres. participle as adjective describing *woman*
9. hoping (that he would be invited to speak at the meeting)—present participle as an adjective describing *Brett*
10. am suggesting—present participle as verb
11. was ordered—past participle as verb
12. working (as fast as possible)—present participle as adjective describing *William*
13. (after) listening—gerund in prepositional phrase
14. (always) suggesting (simplistic solutions)—present participle as adjective describing *David*
15. Angered (by the lack of progress in contract negotiations)—past participle as adjective describing *members*

Exercise 15
Identifying Subject and Verb
1. Mr. Gordon—will make
2. manager—fired (*planning to make major changes* is a present participle as adjective here describing *manager*)
3. factors—are
4. person—will get (*who has enrolled in the course* is an adjective clause describing *person*—ignore the verb in this clause)

5. we—can process
6. you (understood)—get
7. argument—did impress (remove the adverb *not)*
8. we—can guarantee
9. we—are losing
10. I—believe
11. investment—was (LV)
12. profits—have declined
13. supervisor—will change
14. we—hope
15. Tom—will finish, will arrange
16. problems—are expected
17. supervisors—endorse
18. we—will create
19. you (understood)—refer

Exercise 16

Subject/Verb Agreement
1. has (Miss Jennings (sing.) has recommended)
2. is (*neither* is always singular, ignore prep phrase)
3. is (ignore prep phrase—subject is *recommendation,* sing.)
4. is (ignore prep phrase, *assistant* is sing.)
5. was (*each* is sing.; ignore prep phrase)
6. has (*either* is sing.; ignore prep phrase)
7. has (firm name is sing.)
8. is (sing. *cost* is the subject of the noun clause)
9. is (*perception* is sing.)

Exercise 17

Pronoun/Antecedent Agreement
1. he/she *(person* is sing.)
2. his/her *(customer* is sing.)
3. his/her *(everyone* is sing.)
4. his/her *(manager* is sing.)
5. his/her *(person* is sing.)
6. our *(all* is plural)
7. her *(woman* is sing.)
8. his/her *(employee* is sing.)
9. his/her *(everyone* is sing.)
10. his/her *(everybody* is sing.)

Exercise 18

Pronoun Forms as Subjects and Objects
1. me
2. I
3. her, him

4. she
5. him
6. her
7. me
8. her
9. He, me
10. I

Exercise 19
Who/Whom

1. whom (They sent *her* to the meeting.)
2. who *(he* will finish the report if Sally leaves early.)
3. whom (Miss Dixon has appointed *her* as our representative.)
4. who *she*, among the staff, has time to...)
5. whom (I rated *her* highly.)
6. who (who is responsible—adjective clause with *who* as the subject—also can reword: *She is responsible...)*
7. who (who came in late—adjective clause with *who* as the subject—also can reword: *she came in late)*
8. whom (whom we hired last year—adjective clause but *whom* isn't the subject—we hired *them* last year.)
9. whom (This announcement applies to *him*.)
10. whom (I just spoke with *him*.)

Exercise 20
Unclear Pronoun Reference

1. A large expenditure will be necessary to construct the new warehouse, but this **warehouse** will enable us to reach several new markets.
2. Some of the pages had footnotes, but these **pages** (or footnotes) were deleted from the final report.
3. Our relocation to the Southwest will require careful planning, but this **move** will be necessary if we are to remain competitive.

Exercise 21
Types of Sentences

1. simple we/are writing
2. simple I/wish
3. compound I/wanted...so...we/stayed
4. simple he/prepared, practiced
5. simple we/will have (despite introductory infinitive phrase, only one SV)
6. complex (When...you/apply) you (understood)/include
7. complex He/terminated (when...results/began)
8. complex (If...Harry/feels) you (understood)/ask
9. complex records/indicate (that...you/are)
10. complex (If...customer/calls) you (understood)/get

11. complex Marty/told...(that) specifications/had been changed
12. compound I/talked...and...she/was

Exercise 22
Dangling Modifiers, Misplaced Modifiers and

Sentence Fragments

1. Dangling modifier—introductory prepositional phrase lacks a subject; must restructure sentence so the word following the comma is the subject of the introductory phrase:

    By following these procedures,**you** will find that the process takes very little time.

2. Dangling modifier—introductory infinitive phrase lacks a subject; must restructure the sentence so that the word following the comma is the subject of the introductory phrase:

    In concluding the report, **Marianne Jones** added recommendations.

3. Misplaced Modifier—*until December 1* belongs with *still a subsidiary of Davidson Corporation.* Move the prepositional phrase so the sentence reads like this.

    Rick Rodgers thought we were still a subsidiary of Davidson Corporation until December 1.

    The sentence could be made more clear by changing *were still* to *would be.*

    Rick Rodgers thought we would be a subsidiary of Davidson Corporation until December 1.

4. Subordinate clause standing alone—add main clause:

    Although Bill had a great deal of difficulty making the new software package work, **he was finally successful.**

5. correct (**not** an introductory phrase; introductory words are a clause, already containing a subject (*I*), so proper subject identification after the comma is not needed)

6. Misplaced Modifier—*often* goes with *threatened.* Move *often* next to the word it modifies.

    Jack often threatened to leave the company.

    or

    Jack threatened often to leave the company.

7. Dangling modifier—introductory adjective phrase lacks a subject; the word following the comma must be who was alert for errors:

   Alert for errors, Bob's secretary caught the mistake.

8. Dangling modifier—introductory infinitive phrase lacks a subject, so the word following the comma must be the subject of this phrase. Who or what is supposed to provide maximum coverage? Either the insurance company or the policy:

   To provide maximum coverage, **the policy** you select must be comprehensive.

9. Subordinate clause standing alone—add main clause:

   Since the report is due in my manager's office two weeks from today, **I began work on it Tuesday night.**

10. Misplaced Modifier—*to all visitors* goes with *was closed* not *renovations:*

    Last month the Capitol was closed to all visitors for renovations.

11. Correct; this sentence does not contain a dangling modifier because the introductory words are a *clause* (already containing a subject) *not* a phrase (missing a subject). Since the introductory words are a clause, the word that immediately follows the comma is not critical.

12. Dangling modifier—introductory participial phrase missing a subject; therefore, the word following the comma must identify who the subject was in the introductory phrase:

    Reaching for the butter, **he** knocked over his water glass.

13. Sentence fragment—*signed by all parties* is a past participial phrase describing *contracts*. The phrase could be turned into a verb by adding *were* before *signed.*

    The contracts **were signed** by all parties.

    A verb could also be added *after* the phrase:

    The contracts, signed by all parties, **were checked** closely by the legal department.

Exercise 23
Comma Usage

1. items in a series (independent clauses)
2. two independent clauses joined by coordinating conjunction *and*
3. two independent clauses joined by coordinating conjunction *but*
4. two independent clauses joined by coordinating conjunction *but*
5. introductory prepositional phrase

6. two independent clauses joined by coordinating conjunction *and*
7. introductory prepositional phrase
8. introductory prepositional phrase
9. introductory subordinate clause
10. items in a series (infinitives)
11. two independent clauses joined by coordinating conjunction *but*
12. introductory prepositional phrase
13. noun in direct address
14. nonessential appositive
15. nonessential adjective clause
16. noun in direct address
17. two equal-ranking adjectives before a noun
18. noun in direct address; introductory subordinate clause
19. two independent clauses joined by coordinating conjunction *but*
20. nonessential appositive
21. nonessential appositive
22. introductory (present) participial phrase
23. introductory prepositional phrase
24. parenthetical word (would be a linking adverb if *however* had been preceded and followed by independent clauses)
25. parenthetical expression
26. introductory single word
27. parenthetical word (would be a linking adverb if *therefore* had been preceded and followed by an independent clause)
28. set off both city and state with commas within a sentence
29. parenthetical word (would be a linking adverb if *nevertheless* had been preceded and followed by an independent clause)
30. introductory infinitive phrase

Exercise 24
Semicolon and Comma Usage

1. Payment is due within 30 days of the billing date; you can, however, save 2% by paying within 10 days.
2. Sue gave an excellent summary to her presentation, but it was too long.
3. In light of current legalities, however, we cannot make specific comments about previous employees.
4. Sandra Holden was not suited to personnel work;therefore,she was transferred to sales.
5. The meeting began at 8 A.M.; she didn't arrive until 8:30.
6. no additional punctuation is needed
7. We like to hold conferences in San Francisco; it is an interesting city.
8. David and Marjorie split the assignment, and they worked overtime to complete it.
9. Our committee consists of David Anderson, Personnel; Mary Brown, Accounting; and Tom Briscott, Marketing.

10. no additional punctuation is needed—this is **not** a compound sentence even though it contains a *but*. The words after *but* are not a complete thought—the subject is missing. Unless the subject is actually printed, consider it a simple sentence—*one* thought, not two.

11. Because 200 well-qualified candidates applied for the position, the selection process was very difficult.

Exercise 25
Comma, Colon, and Semicolon Usage

1. The following furniture was ordered: two tables, three desks, four chairs, and four printers.
2. In order to graduate, all students are required to complete courses in English, mathematics, accounting, and computer science.
3. This drawer contains basic office supplies: letterhead, envelopes, printer paper, stamps, and a stapler.
4. Only four people failed to attend the sales meeting: Paula Jacobs, Stan Martin, Georgia Gibson, and Monica Rodgers.
5. Please tell Marge that I will keep my 10:30 A.M. appointment; however, I will be unable to keep my 2:30 P.M. appointment.

Exercise 26
Parentheses

1. The projected figures are optimistic. (See page 4.)
2. correct
3. We have held conferences in three major cities (Los Angeles, New York, and Chicago).
4. The recent newspaper article ("The Latest in Computer Technology") was mentioned at yesterday's meeting.
5. Someone from the IRS (Internal Revenue Service) called three times yesterday.
6. correct

Exercise 27
Underlining and Quotation Marks

1. The San Jose Mercury-News interviewed several high-tech company presidents in last Monday's edition.
2. I have been subscribing to PC World for two years.
3. I read three times "Understanding Difficult People" in this month's issue of Psychology Today.
4. Since it was my job to write the new policy, I studied carefully the article entitled "How to Write Effective Policies and Procedures."
5. A summary of the book was presented in The New York Times, The Los Angeles Herald, and the San Francisco Chronicle.
6. Many people misspell *accommodate*. Note: place the period at the end **inside** the end quotation mark.

Exercise 28
Apostrophe Usage
1. anybody's
2. everyone's
3. hour's
4. weeks'
5. minutes
6. company's
7. Reynolds' (*desk* is implied at the end)
8. men's
9. weeks
10. company's
11. hour's
12. clerks'
13. firm's
14. manager's
15. John's
16. manager's
17. couches; women's
18. businesses
19. computer's
20. clerks'
21. It's
22. its
23. Whose
24. who's
25. their
26. its
27. Your
28. you're
29. It's; whose
30. Your; it's
31. Jim's (suggestions)
32. There
33. companies
34. its
35. yours; hers

Exercise 29
Hyphenation
1. first-class
2. state-of-the-art
3. high-level
4. self-serving
5. one-step

6. long-time
7. take-it-or-leave-it
8. ten-hour
9. award-winning
10. color-coordinated
11. two- to five-year (note the space before *to*)
12. ten-page
13. one-hour
14. four-month
15. face-to-face
16. 12-person
17. Denver-based
18. do-it-yourself
19. much-needed
20. on-the-job
21. one-time

Exercise 30
Capitalization

1. The chairperson of the committee is Jeremy Ross, Vice-President of Finance.
2. The south side of the parking lot is being resurfaced today.
3. On Monday morning, Mr. Cordasco will review the document with all department managers.
4. This instrument was originally invented by a French physician.
5. The standard Ford bumper jack is a portable mechanism for raising the front or rear of a car.
6. All companies would like to see more communication courses offered at the local colleges.
7. The Environmental Protection Agency has made a great deal of progress in that area since 1975.
8. Why don't you write to the Consumer Affairs Department?
9. The forklift operator on each shift will direct people out of the building through the loading dock, should a fire occur.
10. Wang Laboratories has been in business for over 30 years.
11. We have had sales problems in the South this quarter.
12. Our guest speaker is Professor Robert Rodriguez from the Accounting Department at Windham College.
13. Company holidays do not include Flag Day.
14. Our invited guest had a great deal to say about the Reagan Era.
15. There was an interesting article on laser technology in last month's issue of <u>PC Computing</u>.
16. Please make me a copy of the article, "Trends in Computing: Applications for the '90s."
17. Ten Thousand Dollars seems like a lot of money for this equipment.
18. TCX Corporation currently has the majority of market share.

19. We took the visiting vice-president to a European restaurant for dinner.
20. I would like to order 20 copies of the book, <u>A Guide to Better Business Management</u>.

Exercise 31
Number Usage
1. Twenty-six
2. 17
3. Eleven
4. 24, 12, 4
5. 16, 25
6. 25, five-pound
7. 5%
8. Twenty-five percent
9. 200
10. August 6
11. $500,000
12. 4%

Exercise 32
Confusing Words
1. accept
2. except
3. affected
4. effects
5. effect
6. effects
7. number
8. number
9. amount
10. farther
11. further
12. Fewer
13. fewer
14. morals
15. moral
16. morale
17. Personnel
18. personal
19. Principal
20. principles
21. principal
22. principal
23. Principles